Bridie Jabour is the opinion editor at *Guardian Australia*. She is the author of the novel *The Way Things Should Be*, which was released in the UK as *My Not So Functional Family*.

TRIVIAL GRIEVANCES

TRIVIAL GRIEVANCES

On the contradictions, myths and misery of your 30s

BRIDIE JABOUR

HarperCollins*Publishers*

HarperCollinsPublishers
Australia • Brazil • Canada • France • Germany • Holland • Hungary
India • Italy • Japan • Mexico • New Zealand • Poland • Spain • Sweden
Switzerland • United Kingdom • United States of America

First published in Australia in 2021
by HarperCollins*Publishers* Australia Pty Limited
Level 13, 201 Elizabeth Street, Sydney NSW 2000
ABN 36 009 913 517
harpercollins.com.au

A catalogue record for this book is available from the National Library of Australia.

ISBN 978 1 4607 5949 3 (paperback)
ISBN 978 1 4607 1311 2 (ebook)
ISBN 978 1 4607 8910 0 (audiobook)

Cover design by Andy Warren, HarperCollins Design Studio
Cover images: Woman with pillows by Julia Buruleva/stocksy.com/2592676;
    sunglasses by shutterstock.com
Author photograph by Anna Turner
Typeset in Sabon LT Std by Kirby Jones
Printed and bound in Australia by McPherson's Printing Group
The papers used by HarperCollins in the manufacture of this book are a natural,
recyclable product made from wood grown in sustainable plantation forests. The fibre
source and manufacturing processes meet recognised international environmental
standards, and carry certification.

For Philomena and Christopher –
you were great parents. Still are, really.

And for Corah, my fellow smart girl.

Contents

1. *Whatever the work is, do it well – not for the boss but for yourself.*
2. *You make the job; it doesn't make you.*
3. *Your real life is with us, your family.*
4. *You are not the work you do; you are the person you are.*

– Toni Morrison

'You are past your prime.'

– My Ma

Chapter one

I was recently at dinner with a group of loose acquaintances of a similar age to celebrate the birthday of a woman I had met ten years earlier at university. She was turning 31.

Also at the table were a divorcee, a single woman, a mother, a woman who had been dating her boyfriend for a few months, and a newlywed. The mood was flat.

The divorcee had been dating a new man for two years and she didn't know where it was going. 'He doesn't understand the fertility issues I have. He says he wants a baby, but I try to talk to him about *when* and he says we don't have to talk about that yet.'

The single woman had gone to a café that morning to have breakfast with a guy she met on a dating app. 'He just didn't show up. I wasn't even that excited to meet him, but he couldn't even be bothered showing up. Breakfast was his idea too. It's always something. I don't even really want a boyfriend, but what else should I be doing with my time?'

The mother's lament was a classic too. She had already drunk three glasses of wine to most of the table's one. 'I didn't appreciate what I had when I had it – the freedom, the lack of direction. I actually just want my lack of structure back. I don't think I thought enough about what having a child was going to be like.'

The woman with the new boyfriend began talking about work. 'I started this job because I thought it was a good opportunity, but now this is my actual job, not just a stepping stone to something else.'

The newlywed described her wedding as an anti-climax. 'I had been looking forward to it for so long! And now it's done, I don't know what I should look forward to next. My job has become so uninteresting; it feels like everything has become so uninteresting.'

Different miseries, to be sure – so different it was actually barely a coherent conversation, more just a series of monologues. But I had met this group of women a few times over the past year, and they were not like this 12 months ago.

Turning 30 had been such a novelty. It was like we were doing it for a laugh – look at us pretending to have a 'milestone birthday', look at us with our gold '30' balloons and our grown-up parties in proper venues rather than in our backyards. We were parroting what we thought people should say at age 30, with a nod and a wink. In our hearts, however, we weren't 30. We certainly didn't *feel* 30. To us, 30 was a lark.

The realisation that time was indeed passing was a slow one. Did it matter you had spent the weekend with your nose hovering over a $10 note? Did it matter this relationship you were in was just *fine*? Did it matter that you'd turned down that job because it was in Canberra (yuck)?

Well, yes. It mattered. Every evening spent scrolling, every deadline missed, the texts not returned, the money blown. It's all been adding up to something. Your life.

At 31, I had been in a great new job for more than a year. I had published my novel 18 months earlier and given birth to my first baby just before that. Yet I had been experiencing a certain kind of tedium for a little while.

I had thought my dissatisfaction was perhaps a symptom of my brattiness. There had been no parties in my honour lately, no announcements to make with a satisfied air of self-deprecation ('some personal news'). Intellectually, I knew I was not special, but in my heart I still loved the applause. I wondered if maybe I was experiencing depression for the first time in my life.

Then I thought it was more likely my feet were getting a bit itchy.

Entering my 30s I was a mother, had a great job, had even published a book. What more could I want? But this gnawing feeling continued to grow. Couldn't I be doing more? Should I have done something different instead? Like become an astronaut? I felt petulant, ungrateful.

But when I finally lifted up my head and looked around, I realised I wasn't the only one. Surveying people of a similar age revealed I wasn't just being a brat. Everyone seemed to be struck down with this same malaise. Whether they were my close friends or acquaintances, lived in another hemisphere or had never left the state, every 31-year-old I spoke to seemed to be in a state of ennui.

I wrote about it for the *Guardian*. The article, 'The millennials at 31: Welcome to the age of misery', was viewed more than half a million times. The response was like a tsunami of discontent.

'During my 30's and now I have to endure second thoughts about everything; questions such as if it could be better if I had made a different choice ? or if I could do anything to change it, and these thoughts are beyond annoying yet very addictive ... at least your article made me feel not special; For some strange reason I thought I was the only one on [sic] misery,' a man wrote to me from California.

From a woman in Australia: 'I have three children – 31, 34 and 35. None of them own a home or have children at least yet. They are all in "good" jobs but I see stresses I never even realised existed when I was their age. Life is more complicated and continuity is less assured than it was.'

One man simply said: 'A PATHETIC REPORTER WRITING ABOUT A PATHETIC GENERATION FFS!'

A woman in England told me she and her friends had been talking about the piece for days. 'OMG you reached into my brain and put everything I've been struggling with the last few months in writing,' she said.

We're not the first cohort to experience a crisis. To experience the passing of time. And by passing of time, I mean the dawning realisation that time is finite, and we might have already wasted a lot. We used to have time to burn. But it was a late blooming into misery.

While Gen Xers and the boomers before us had these realisations by 25, for millennials the prolonged adolescence that was our 20s had delayed this type of self-reflection. And the hangover seemed more severe.

People who have spent years striving and hustling are suddenly questioning it all. If they are not happy being defined by their job, then what do they want to be defined by? Friends? Family? Apartment? Character? A job seems the easiest when you really start grappling with it. You don't have to like the person you are if you are defined by your job. Of course, your job is also never going to love you back.

It is an old compulsion to try to impose a narrative on our lives, especially when looking for meaning in our existence. But life does have a natural progression, a natural flow that millennials ought to have simply participated in, and many feel it's not flowing as it should. Many felt there were certain things that should have fallen into place by their 30s. Namely: partner, shelter, job and probably children. Yet there have never been more single people in their 30s globally, there's a housing affordability crisis in pretty much every western country, and in many industries, the career progression that existed for many decades has simply disappeared.

What was happening was a good old-fashioned identity crisis. But an identity crisis in a unique set of social and economic circumstances. Precarious work, delayed baby-making, rising singledom, a heating planet, loss of religion and increased unstable housing mean this generation is facing old problems – who am I? – in a different world. And if that weren't enough, we now have to contend with a pandemic placing radical restrictions on modern life.

Just like the lobster surprised to find itself boiling to death, in hindsight, the signs of our impending misery had been there all along.

***

The growing uptake of astrology by millennials has been documented by the *New Yorker*, the *Guardian*, the *LA Times*, the *Washington Post* and, of course, by millennials themselves on Instagram. The enthusiasm with which we had embraced astrology would have told us, if we had paused to think about it for a second, everything that we needed to know about ourselves. We were clinging onto life rafts made of horoscopes to try to eke meaning out of our lives and the illusion of control.

We didn't discover astrology, but we are the first to be downloading daily horoscope apps by the million and texting to friends, 'Sorry I'm not ready yet, but you know I'm a Scorpio.'

It's generally agreed that uncertain economic and political times drive people's interest in astrology – the first newspaper astrology column was commissioned in the British *Sunday Express* just after the stock market crash in 1930 – but I think there is more to this renaissance. I am a walking cliché when it comes to horoscopes and tarot reading.

My mother grew up in Northern Ireland and when I say she is Catholic, people nod in understanding: 'Oh yeah, I grew up Catholic too.' But the difference between an Irish Catholic and an Australian Catholic is like the difference between Roger Federer and a two-year-old playing with a tennis ball. The toddler lacks the full-body commitment.

I went to mass every single Sunday, and many other times during the week, until I left home. No discussion about my attendance was permitted. Mum still goes almost every day of the week. When I pushed my first baby into the world, I lifted my exhausted head from the bed and watched Mum pull out a vial of holy water from her pocket and bless my son before I had even held him. That's Irish Catholic, baby.

I quickly lapsed as an adult and, in my late 20s, a friend sitting next to me at the movies on New Year's Day showed me what she was reading. It was a 4000-word horoscope for the month, published by astrologer Susan Miller.

Later that day, I idly looked mine up, and I have read my horoscope every single month since, convinced that Susan had predicted various events like my job change, my friend meeting her partner, book deals and even when my mum found out I was pregnant.

(Astrology also explains the misery so many in their early 30s experience with a phenomenon called 'Saturn return', when Saturn returns to the same place in the sky that it occupied at the moment of a person's birth. The influence of Saturn return tends to start when a person is in their late 20s.)

At 31, not yet realising the universality of my quarter-ish life crisis, I turned to a tarot card reader. Along with the constant low thrum of terror about the future, I felt stuck professionally and had started to panic. Was I doing enough? Were my career peaks already behind me? Was anything exciting going to happen to me again, ever?

As she laid out the cards face down, she listened to my fretting about my job and how my forthcoming book would do in the UK. Then she turned over a card, and the first thing she said was: 'You need to look the fuck around.'

She told me I needed to appreciate what I had already achieved, that I had actually done quite a lot and what I needed was to step back and enjoy it. An extremely easy thing that all of us are very good at doing regularly.

'You're like a therapist!' I said as she flipped another card.

'The cards are the therapist,' she responded.

It's easy to argue astrology is a simple replacement for organised religion, which we are fleeing in droves, but I don't think that is quite right. There are few devotees of astrology who subscribe to it in the holy and life-ruling way people are devoted to religion. Astrology does not give people's lives meaning the way that religion does. It's difficult to ascertain how much of astrology we truly believe. We want to appear to believe in it as a joke, especially on the internet. But what we have actually found in astrology is a way to talk about ourselves in a deeply serious way while safe under the cloak of irony.

In the *Guardian*, Stephanie Convery wrote about an academic friend of hers who had once used tarot cards to think through problems:

> she ... found the cards soothing and unexpectedly helpful ... It wasn't about fate or fortune-telling in a crystal ball kind of way; it was about having a tool for ordering the disorder, a foil against which she could hold complex life events and see them from a different angle.

When I went to the tarot card reader, I believed what she told me. I was stressing over things that did not need to be stressed over and I needed to appreciate more what I already had. I could talk through my anxieties without worrying about seeming vain and petty. We were both talking to the cards, after all. This wasn't quite real.

In a self-deprecating, hyper-competitive age, tarot card reading can be a good way to talk through your issues without paying too much for it. To confide in someone who can tell you to 'look the fuck around', but without having to do anything embarrassing like being earnest.

As any good astrologist will tell you, the stars don't dictate your future. They tell you the circumstances you're working in; it's up to you what you do with them. Which is pretty standard, self-evident advice.

***

Astrology may help us maintain an illusion of control, but nowhere else do we see such a neat meeting between how we want the world to see us and how we actually are than in the complicated and vaguely scientific skincare routines embraced by millennials across the world.

In a time when we talk about body positivity and wellness rather than diets, skincare has become an acceptable way to obsess about how you look. You get to spend money while distracting yourself from the fact that, while you can brighten your skin with the right combination of retinol and vitamin C, you're still stuck with the face you have.

Skincare has grown to more than 25 per cent of the beauty and personal care market globally and the business consulting firm Grand View Research projects it to be worth $183.3 billion by 2025. Glossier became a billion-dollar company within five years of launching off the back of the skincare and 'natural look' trend; and Australian Zoë Foster Blake's 'clean' skincare range Go-To is in Mecca Cosmetica stores, is expanding into the American market, and sells more than a product a minute.

In 2021, Reddit's 'skincare addiction' sub has 1.1 million subscribers, more than double the already huge number of 420,000 in 2018.

As academic Efrat Tseëlon puts it, it's part of 'the fetishisation of emotions, desires and values into material objects'. In this case, equal parts wanting to stay young and attractive even if we don't articulate it that way, as well as the relief of being able to do something – whether that's double cleansing or exfoliating – and see the results of our effort. Our glowing skin is material evidence that we can impact something, *anything*.

Our spiralling political climate, as well as the bonfire that is our actual climate, have been cited as reasons for our newfound passion for skincare regimes, because these regimes are a means by which we can wrest back some control. The size and complexity of political problems, coupled with our alienation from them, makes self-care the limit of many people's capacity to take responsibility for their world.

But as Krithika Varagur pointed out in the *Outline*, in a type of blasphemy in some circles, don't we all have friends with strict and expensive skincare regimes who ... do not have good skin? Well, she says, the point isn't good skin, but the regime, the relentless drive to always be improving ourselves.

But it's so boring to constantly be thinking of the ways you are being trapped by (I'm rolling my eyes and doing inverted commas with my fingers) 'capitalism' and how stupid it is to care about the things you care about, like how your face looks.

The same *Outline* article goes on to lecture:

Real, flawed women have real, flawed skin – it's fine. Your skin, by the way, naturally protects against diseases and foreign bodies, regulates your body temperature, prevents water loss, insulates your soft tissues, synthesizes Vitamin D, etc., etc. Give it some credit.

As I read that paragraph, I feel myself regressing to my teenage self. 'Okay, Mum,' I sigh petulantly. 'Skin does lots of boring useful stuff and I am a victim of capitalism. But I still *like* doing it.'

It's much easier to tell me 'real, flawed women have real, flawed skin' than to actually *be* the 'real, flawed woman'.

We don't know if our landlords are going to let us stay in our places in a year, or what job we are going to have in two years, but there is clinical evidence that AHAs will make our skin look better. There is comfort in the ritual, consolation in the regime. It's an indulgence that won't send us broke and the sight of various pastel-coloured bottles in my bathroom is quite soothing.

Astrology and skincare are both things to do while we wait for our life to start. While we wait for the life that was supposed to have started already.

They are not only taken up by people as they approach their 30s, but the fanaticism with which this demographic embraces them points to a deeper discontent.

We're not just doing this for fun. We are trying to feel better.

***

Skincare and astrology may be salves for our existential crisis, but a salve is not a solution. Looking for a solution to this crisis of misery at times feels like looking for a solution to 'being human'. So far, the only two I have come up with are:

1. Become very grave and take life *very* seriously.
2. Take an ironic posturing: 'Life isn't going the way I want, oh well, I'm not special, what does it matter?'

What has produced the kind of person who experiences life as quite overwhelming but also feels detached from it? I am aware this dichotomy exists in this essay, and it also exists in myself.

It is true a lot of millennials' lives are harder than they ought to be, but a lot of people in their 30s also struggle to feel satisfied with the decisions they have made. They don't just need to be patted on the back and have their tears wiped away. Part of the reason people get so hurt is nobody tells them the truth.

The truth is that life is hard for a large swathe of us. There are things that are more difficult for us than the two previous generations. But, in the context of the history of humankind, which is a fairly big context to be fair, things *are* better. I'd much rather be a woman born in 1988 than a woman born in the 1950s like many boomers. I don't know a single disabled person, Black person or queer person who would rather be born in the 1950s than 1988.

There is so much about life that millennials find exhausting. They struggle to make judgments then feel secure in those judgments. They burn out. They put huge expectations on themselves then panic about small things, such as whether to cancel plans with a friend that evening. Everything, from small thoughts about how you see yourself to important massive social movements, comes from a place of 'I'm sick of this, but I don't know how to change it' and it's a big blow to the ego to admit that. Even when people try to tease out what is at the centre of these dilemmas, it can be dismissed as 'middle-class' concerns.

'Middle class' has become a shorthand for boring, ill-thought-out, parochial, daft, stale, undergraduate. Too basic to bother with. I kid you not, I have seen a conversation about whether people drank water as kids hijacked by the comment 'drinking water as a kid is quite middle class'.

Being able to talk about and recognise class is very important. What many of us don't admit when talking about the class divide is that, secretly, we feel quite superior to our rich contemporaries. Especially if they grew up in the city, which they almost always did.

It is tough, at times, to move to the city and succeed there with no money and no connections, but I am pretty sure all people who talk about their working-class backgrounds privately think they have much more substance than the wealthy. There is something steely about us, unknowable. But we really want you to know it.

Oh, your mum is buying you a house in Sydney?

Well, I grew up in a family of seven in a three-bedroom house which at one point had 11 people living in it. My brother and I got so over living in such cramped quarters, we cleaned out the shed and moved into it. When Dad saw the set-up, he moved in there too.

You may be rich but I'm interesting! Also, I'm middle class now, and I love it.

Anyway, when people dismiss something as middle class – say, having a weird crisis about being in your 30s – they're saying, 'I am far more interesting than you because

I'm not middle class' or, more likely, they're saying, 'I'm middle class and I'm boring so I'm trying to pretend I'm more interesting than that.'

Or maybe that's just me. I don't think I've ever felt inferior. Self-conscious, briefly, when I arrived in Sydney and the class divide became more stark to me than it had ever been. But what am I going to do? Trade in my massive, eccentric family for cash?

Often when things are dismissed as middle class, the implicit comparison is not to the uber-rich but to the working class, upon which a cartoon-like reverence has been bestowed. In this discourse, the working class are seen as knowing what real life is about, as being intolerant of bullshit. If you believe people on Twitter, they all grew up working class, but somehow aren't anymore. Part of this longing to belong to the working class is an ideological Left infatuated with their own oppression, and another part of it is pure fetishisation. It is, after all, mostly middle-class people who dismiss concepts or other people as 'middle class'. There is nothing wrong with the middle class, nobody stupider or not as human for being in it. There are middle-class people who are tedious, vain and oblivious, and there are working-class people who are tedious, vain and oblivious. There are absolutely a lot of rich people who are tedious, vain and oblivious.

It is lazy to dismiss anything or anyone just for being 'middle class', but I do not think the current collective identity crisis is confined there either. How much we are all working or not working, whether to have children or not, intimate relationships, what defines us: these are things that preoccupy people across class, race, sexuality and gender as they enter their 30s. What we may need, as well as a dose of hard truth, is creative solutions to our malaise.

Are we the first people to ever feel this way?

By the time you get to your early 30s, the broad outlines of your life are probably apparent.

You may make some new friends, change jobs and move house. But you know who your close circle of friends are, you're likely to remain in the industry your career is being built in, and you live in the country that you will most likely stay in.

So if you're unhappy, it can feel difficult to change because you are, at this point, either locked in or locked out of a certain kind of life.

The locked in/locked out phenomenon is studied by academic Oliver Robinson, who has taken a particular interest in the 'quarter-life crisis', an existential malaise definitely not invented by millennials, but perhaps being perfected by us.

According to Robinson, 'locked in' means you see all of your options shutting down around you. You chose this job, so you can't pursue that one; you are with this person, so you may have missed the chance to be with someone different, perhaps more attractive and/or richer. You've decided to live in this city, so you probably will never live in that town. Your obligations have mounted, you have bills that have to be paid, welcome to your ordinary life.

If you're locked out, you don't even have a job to worry about being the wrong one, or a partner to fret over. If you're locked out, then you feel like those things are out of your grasp; you don't even have the luxury of worrying if you have made the wrong decision.

Being locked in used to be the classic existential crisis, but the unhappiness I have witnessed is much more to do with being locked out. It is a larger cohort of millennials than previous generations who are locked out of careers, stable housing and, because of that, even locked out of starting families.

The misery of people in their early 30s is neatly distilled in the binary.

***

One of the lazy myths constantly evoked about millennials is that we are convinced of our specialness. Raised with participation awards, so the stereotype goes, we believe in

19

our own hype, that we can't fail, that we are deserving of success and admiration.

An even older trope is that each generation thinks they are the first to discover things such as sex, music and self-excavation. By the time you are 31, you are not supposed to think about this stuff anymore. But we do. I do.

I had long theorised that we've had a prolonged adolescence. I assumed that because a lot of adult markers had been delayed, we had experienced our 20s as a kind of extension of our teens, figuring ourselves out, not needing to take on responsibilities that previous generations had from an earlier age.

Well, you know what they say about assuming. When you assume, you ... ring three people with actual expertise to find out just how wrong you are.

'Something which is probably uncomfortable for all humans, despite thinking in our adolescence that we are cool and edgy and different from our parents, is that the horrible truth is we really do absorb a lot more of the messages about what we can do, what we can't do, what we should do, what we shouldn't do [than we think].'

Who said that? Socrates?

No, it was Emily Dowling, in the first 65 seconds of talking to me about the supposedly unique crisis of today's 31-year-olds.

Dowling is a psychologist based in Sydney, who sees a lot of people in their late 20s. While she has 'reservoirs of sympathy' for them – a direct quote – the prolonged adolescence we have just experienced may not be as deeply unique as I first thought. It may not even exist.

Dowling is with me on the economic and social factors that have delayed adulthood for many, but the crisis I think it has created – 'What do I want to do with my life? Who do I want to be?' – has been felt by many people before.

'The simplest thing to say is society is changing. Rapidly. We've known for decades people have been delaying marriage and delaying having children, and we are now looking at a time where there doesn't seem to be as much wealth. So who knows what will happen?' she says.

What she thinks is going to happen is a reduction in living standards and lifestyle compared with previous generations. I think that is already happening.

Gen Xers graduated from university in a recession, but when most of them were in their early 30s the economy had stabilised and the six-year property boom of 2013 was a faraway twinkle in their eyes. The workforce was much less casualised and automation had not yet kicked into gear.

Now, Dowling says, the main things she sees her patients grappling with in their early 30s are housing and career.

The obsession with property can seem very privileged, mostly because it is. If you have a house, you are freer to spend your time worrying about outfits, petty squabbles, the kind of person you want to be, general happiness.

(Not to say that people without property don't have the same sorts of worries. I once met a psychologist who went into Syrian refugee camps in Lebanon. She had expected to be counselling young people on their trauma, which she did, but she also spent a surprising amount of time talking to her clients about whether a certain someone was in love with them or not.)

When you're grappling with how to own property, in Australia especially, you're grappling with how to have a home. It's about having somewhere to live where you can hang a picture without being penalised, where you don't have to have a stranger come through every few months to check how clean and tidy you are, and where you cannot be kicked out on a whim because the owner thinks they can make more money with the property in a different way.

When we stress about property, it's not about wanting the best McMansion; it's about feeling safe in a home that is yours. It's about knowing where you are going to live and make your life. This is a situation that could be greatly improved with more rights for renters, but, until that happens, owning property is the focus.

'There's a lot of discussion about how millennials are appalling because they live with their parents for a lot longer. Which I find fascinating, because when we look at human history, that's happened before,' Dowling says. 'This idea that "When I reach early adulthood I get to move out to a space of my own where I have my own room, my own bathroom, my own kitchen and I get my own living space and I get to control all of that and my parents get to get me out of their hair and go on their European river cruise" – I'm not saying it's wrong, but it's a sign of aching wealth. Aching, aching wealth and resources.'

Merely having the choice of moving out or staying at home is a sign of aching wealth and resources. One of my closest friends, Lee, grew up in a hippy community on the fringes of a country town. Her parents were nurses, so she wasn't poor, but there wasn't a lot of spare cash. Her parents still live in that country town in Queensland.

A couple of years ago, during a particularly tedious time at work for her, she started dating an intimidatingly intelligent (well, we thought so at the time) man who was big on not letting your job 'morally corrupt' you, or just generally suck your soul out of your body.

He would often tell her to just quit her job and figure out what she wanted to do. It was a revelation to us, and we would talk about his suggestion in awed tones. 'It truly is such a different way of looking at it,' we would say. 'Why don't we just quit? Maybe there is another way to live our lives.'

After he and Lee had split up and he had headed to Europe to fulfil himself creatively, it dawned on Lee and me why we hadn't just simply thought of that before. His parents still lived in the four-bedroom house in the inner east of Sydney in which he grew up. He moved out of his apartment and stored his things at his parents' house at no cost. When he eventually came back to Australia, he would just crash rent-free at his parents' house while re-establishing himself in Sydney.

If Lee and I decided to pack up and move overseas, we would have to sell our stuff or pay for storage while we were gone. Then when we came home, we would have to figure out how to re-establish ourselves from northern New South Wales or north Queensland. We'd probably never get back to where we are now. We had pretty much clawed our way here.

Aside from the 'aching wealth' Dowling sees in some people's assumptions of how young people should be living, she sees the actual results of these expectations weighing on the shoulders of people in their 30s.

'I'm certainly seeing a lot of anxiety, huge amounts of anxiety, and anxiety, by definition, is the result of a perceived stressor. I see a lot of alcohol use and drug use, which I would say is soothing anxiety. [I also see] a fair bit of consumerism,' she says.

'People are not going home on public transport "to my house with my husband and my children like my mother did. So what do I do instead? I wear cooler clothes, which I've bought online, and I go out drinking with the girls and we go to fabulous wine bars. My grandparents wouldn't even know what a wine bar is. I go there all the time, because I'm different to them."'

I recognise the routine instantly. That routine was very fun for me, I interject.

'Of course it is [fun], but it's a different way people are living their lives. It depends on how much money they have, but it can be a way people are coping when a couple of generations ago, at age 32, a high proportion of people would be going home to put kids to bed. If you're in your early 30s and you don't have a house and a husband and kids to put to bed, what do you do? And the answer can be [to go to] a wine bar.'

It turns out the wine bar is not going to make you happy. It may make you happy for a night, but it is not going to make you a happy person. I remember how fun it was, but I also remember how bored I eventually became of it, how routine it became.

It still feels kind of silly, though, that *en masse* this is what our collective freak-out could be about. How we want to be in the world.

It was a personal crisis that was exacerbated by the global health pandemic. Briefly people were preoccupied with the really essential stuff – livelihoods were stripped away and we contemplated our parents' mortality as well as our own. COVID-19 took away wine bars, took away the office; it even took away hugging our friends. For a lot of people, it sealed their decision about not having kids. It locked out many, many people.

But in relative terms, in this country we still have enormous wealth, even when we feel like we don't. The healthcare is good, mostly. There are enormous privileges.

We are currently in the midst of crises that before 2020 we could only dimly fathom. Surely we can also survive some misery. How does Dowling treat this dread in her patients?

'A lot of it is about thinking, "What did you think your life would look like? What did you want your life to look like?" and acknowledging that, but then really working out what is reality and trying to work out what can you do with the resources you have,' she says.

I ask my next question tentatively: 'How long does it take you to get people to accept that?'

'It's a constant acceptance, it is absolutely constant. Another group in society who are doing the same thing are people in aged care. Where your reality may be: you are extremely physically unable, your eyesight is going, you have low-level chronic pain. And within that, within your resources, what can you do to live your values and have the best possible life you can have, while you're ageing? It's not easy. It's not easy.'

Learning not to be too hard on yourself is key to learning resilience in your 30s. You can't be happy all of the time; it is not possible. Any time you are thinking, 'Where did I go wrong?', remember that there is no scenario where you think, 'This is the perfect path for me, every decision

I made was correct.' There is no path where you are not wondering about other choices you could have made. It's not just in your 30s you will need these lessons either; it's going to be forever.

'[These questions have] hit every single person who didn't die aged 62 of a heart attack. Those are your options: drop dead or learn to live with your body diminished. Try to find joy, try to find meaning, try to find value within the resources that you have. It never stops.'

***

When I ask Oliver Robinson if he thinks 31-year-olds are more miserable now than at any other time in recent history, he is unequivocal.

'No.'

Robinson is a senior lecturer for psychology in the School of Human Sciences at the University of Greenwich in London. He is cautious when we first start talking over Skype.

'I think that they [millennials] are faced with a radically different existential situation than people in their early 30s in different generations,' he says. 'But I think that the differences are a complex mixture of good things and challenges. Now, I don't think I'd be confident to say that they are more miserable, no.'

Robinson has spent years researching the quarter-life crisis which can tip into one's 30s. He says the 'substantial social revolution' we have been unwittingly living through for the past few decades has begun to plateau, mostly because parenthood cannot be put off indefinitely. The social revolution has been the upheaval of previous social norms such as only having sex within a marriage, getting married very soon in adulthood, having children fairly quickly after and women staying in the home within that set-up. Marriage and children have become increasingly delayed but biologically people are still forced to make the children decision by 40, usually. They can't delay beyond that.

'Most people who've lived through a period [of revolution] don't recognise that they've lived through that revolution,' he says. 'But historians will look back on [this period] as an extraordinary time of change.'

Even before the global health pandemic, the rate of social change was dizzying.

He dismisses my theory of a prolonged adolescence, though, instead talking about a new distinct life stage of emerging adulthood.

'It's an exploratory pre-settling-down, and what one tends to see in that stage of life is a weird paradoxical mix of peaks and troughs, such that you're at the peak of life in many ways, in terms of positive good things. But it's also the peak in terms of all sorts of problems as well. I mean, pretty much every bad thing you can imagine in life, with the exception of dementia, peaks in ages 18 to 30.'

So what 31-year-olds today find themselves emerging from is the very best of times, as well as the very worst of times. You've spent the past decade as free as you will probably ever be, and also perhaps abusing alcohol more than you ever will, losing a friend or two to an untimely death, and dealing with mental-health issues. And probably also being broke.

'There's really nothing special in actuality about hitting 30 or 40. But it feels significant and important, because you feel like you've just done a decade. And you're looking ahead to the next one and doing a bit of a life review. So I do think that hitting 30 means there's a lot of people asking themselves, "Well, in this world of infinite possibility, where I could be with all these different kinds of people, live in different places, do different kinds of jobs, have I made the right choices?"

'Most people want to be loved, they want to feel that they're doing something that's worthwhile, and that life makes sense despite the fact that it's frequently shit.'

***

It is difficult to ascertain how special some people secretly think they are. Hard to get them to admit it, harder still to quantify. I don't think millennials are a particularly coddled generation. Not everyone got participation certificates, as some pundits like to believe, and even if they did I don't think they would have made a particularly deep impression on the psyche.

My suspicion is that most people have felt that they are special, that one day they will be singled out – they are, after all, the protagonist of their life. I think a lot of people are waiting for someone to recognise their secret specialness, waiting for something to happen to them.

This is one of the reasons I think US Representative Alexandria Ocasio-Cortez and actress Meghan Markle were able to look so comfortable when suddenly thrust into global fame. AOC, as she has come to be known, was fighting for something she truly believes in, but she also thought she was the right person for the fight. I think Meghan Markle was also secretly waiting for the big thing to happen, when everyone would see how special she was. And something special did happen to Markle and AOC.

Sure, there's insecurity and low self-esteem, but also deep down there is the whisper, 'I knew someone was going to see it soon. See *me* soon.'

For most of us, though, that doesn't happen. We get to 31 and look around and … this is about it. No global fame, no fated recognition; our mums probably don't even think we are that special anymore. We are just normal people living normal lives. We want meaning in our lives, but a lot of us also want people to see that we are meaningful too. All along we have been secretly believing we are the gripping stars of the theatre of our lives.

Instead we are stuck here, realising our lives are trivial.

Robinson had his own crisis in his late 20s, when he realised he was in the wrong job, and with the wrong woman. He and his girlfriend broke up and he was let go from his corporate job. For a long time, he says, he accepted that money was the goal, but then he discovered a passion for academia – and accepted he would never be rich as a result.

'My parents are very conventional, very nice, but their tolerance of unusualness is very low indeed. I started a band, I started just being far more eccentric and trying lots of strange things and doing all sorts of stuff, and I'm not sure how much they knew about it, to be honest,' he says.

'As I started doing these different things, and got more into music and what have you, some of my more conventional friends just got left behind.'

While Dowling says we basically need to learn to be happy with what we have – certainly true in a lot of cases – Robinson says that misery can actually be a good thing. You can't change your life, or yourself, if you're satisfied.

'Life is such that people very rarely make very substantive changes when they're happy,' he says. 'Happiness as an emotion basically says, "Carry on doing what you're doing."

'Because of the inertia that there is in life where you bed yourself in, to make changes is a massive hassle. Sometimes the only thing that is going to do it for you is feeling really bad. Feeling strong negative emotions is the most powerful motive for change. There's no doubt that I was feeling strong negative emotions at that time, all sorts of strange negative emotions that I was trying to make sense of, and ... I remember now, I just thought: "I can't carry on like this."'

A horrific feeling at the time, but he would not be where he is today if he had thought, 'I will just go on like this.'

'The medical model of being human says it's normal to feel happy and it's bad, dysfunctional, wrong to feel down or anxious. But I would contend to you that it would be extremely odd and inappropriate for someone to feel happy all the time. A tapestry of emotions is appropriate and the bad emotions, their principal message is: "Please change something."

'So it's crucial to have those bad feelings because, as I say, they drive change.'

According to Robinson, being locked in or locked out are the main two reasons for a quarter-life crisis – which technically begins in people's 20s but can certainly be carried into the early 30s.

'Age-wise, locked-out tends to come a bit earlier than locked-in. So, a locked-out crisis for a 30-something would be perhaps initiated by unemployment or a chronic inability to settle into a relationship that's desired,' he says.

'Whatever occurs by way of external changes – let's say someone gets the job or leaves a job, or changes their social circle, or quits the drugs, or moves, or whatever it is they fundamentally change – that's only going to be effective if they make substantial internal changes as well.

'Crisis is always kind of a call to try and change the way that you see the world and the things you aspire towards. And so whatever the resolution is of the crisis, if it's going to resolve, there has to be some sense that who I am inwardly and what I'm doing outwardly are a good fit. That I feel that my life represents me as a person in terms of my values and my deepest aspirations.'

What makes either of these crises more acute, whether it is locked-out or the more bourgeois locked-in, is that they come at a time when you're supposed to be having the best time of your life. Anyone who says life begins at 40 is lying to themselves as much as they are to you. The funnest part is meant to be now! Your sexy, financially independent 30s. So if you're just coming to terms with how mundane life can be, it is particularly bitter to do it at the same time you're supposed to be having all of this fun.

Someone once said:

We spent as much money as we could and got as little for it as people could make up their minds to give us. We were always more or less miserable, and most of our acquaintances were in the same condition. There was a gay fiction among us that we were constantly enjoying ourselves, and a skeleton truth that we never did. To the best of my belief our case in the last aspect was a rather common one.

Famous millennial Charles Dickens wasn't explicitly talking about the 31-year-old malaise when he wrote that in *Great Expectations*, but he's dead now so we can project whatever we want on those words. It's how the extended adolescence that apparently doesn't exist feels; the 'gay fiction' is everywhere I turn.

It is obvious to connect that gay fiction with social media, but of course it's everywhere there too. The gay fiction of constantly having fun, wearing cute outfits, feeling restored in front of vistas of the ocean, adventures while travelling.

Then there is the gay fiction we share with our friends and tell ourselves almost daily. That we are enjoying everything we are participating in. That we aren't terrified. That we have some semblance of control over ourselves and our lives. A gay fiction obscuring the dawning realisation that we might have to accept an ordinary life, and be dissatisfied at least some of the time.

Getting past the gay fiction is learning to live your life within confined horizons, or changing the horizons. But what if the horizons you change are worse than the horizons you have? Ah, but what if it's better? What if, what if. It's a question you will have to learn to live with for the next 50 years, if you're lucky enough to live for another 50 years.

When you find yourselves at the crossroads of being locked out or locked in, no matter your age there is always time to change. Changing doesn't necessarily mean changing your situation; the changing can be to your feelings. That doesn't mean lowering your expectations to a puny life, but being grateful for your puny life.

If you are locked out, that's a harder thing to remedy than being locked in and will require more work. Being locked out of jobs, romantic relationships, a circle of friends – those are difficult things with no easy answer. Nevertheless, the basic options for both being locked in and being locked out are elegant in their simplicity, and very difficult, although possible, to carry out.

If you are locked out, then the smallest foothold is needed. If you can't get a job or proper financial security, remember it is not a reflection upon you. You can work very hard and still come up short; it's how the system operates sometimes.

If you are locked in – feeling trapped in your town, your relationship, your job – it requires courage, but you can change the material circumstances of your life.

An option for both is working on acceptance of your life and figuring out what there is to be grateful for. Taking responsibility for yourself in the knowledge that not everything is your fault, and focusing on what you can control. You are not a failure for feeling hopeless, but you don't have to always feel this way.

Marriage is an empty constitution, and other dumb things I've said

When I was a teenager, I used to proudly declare to anyone who would listen that marriage was an 'empty constitution'. I must have heard the phrase somewhere and thought it sounded supremely cool, though I of course pretended I had come up with it myself. It was only much later, after I had repeated this many, many times, that I realised I had confused 'institution' with 'constitution'.

Throughout my 20s, I was ambivalent about getting married. Part of it was that I felt a little too cool for it, this old-fashioned mainstream ritual, and another part was that I just thought marriage didn't matter.

There are certainly bureaucratic reasons to get married – you never know when automatic next of kin will matter – but it is no longer taboo for a lot of Australians to cohabitate and have children without marriage. You can live together and share finances and be a family without what people love to refer to as the 'bit of paper'.

As I entered my late 20s, suddenly everyone around me, myself included, was getting married. The other major markers of adulthood we had been promised as teens in the early 2000s were not on the horizon. Hardly any of us owned property, or had 'careers' with a simple long-term progression laid out, or had children. But if we remembered to check the letterbox for the one or two bills still being sent via snail mail, there was always a colourful envelope containing multiple cards with bright designs, perhaps a specially commissioned drawing of a happy couple, and questions about dietary preferences – in other words, a wedding invitation – waiting as well. As we approached 30, more and more of these envelopes arrived.

Everyone likes to think they have their own twist on weddings. I heard so often, 'But we didn't have bridesmaids and groomsmen', or 'But we walked down the aisle together', or 'But we had a combined bucks and hens'. Yet it doesn't matter if you wore a blue dress or had ironic vows or did not throw the bouquet, you still got married. There's not much in the modern Anglo western world more old-fashioned than that.

The pull of it can be breathtaking. Yet at the same time it feels a little bit pointless. There are some weird wedding traditions that aren't even that old, like diamond rings and white dresses. (People mistakenly think white was traditionally worn as a symbol of virginity, and while it may have morphed into that, it was in fact a trend started by Queen Victoria. She wore handmade Honiton lace on her wedding day to boost the industry in England and white was the best colour to showcase the lace.)

Millennials are the first generation in the past 120 years in which the majority are not married by their mid-30s. The rates vary around the world, but about 44 per cent of millennials in western countries were married in 2019. At about the same age, 53 per cent of Gen Xers, 61 per cent of boomers and 81 per cent of pre-boomers were married.

***

On 24 March 2020, as part of the first coronavirus lockdown in Australia, Prime Minister Scott Morrison announced a limit of five people at weddings. Within a week, Alyx Gorman's boyfriend proposed to her with a ring he had been designing for a year. Within a month, with the entire country still in lockdown, they got married in front of almost 400 guests watching from Boston, Paris, New York, London and my own unfashionable Sydney suburb.

Alyx, 31, had been raised by communist parents who never married, so she was imbued with what she calls a 'natural scepticism' of it from a young age. But her fiancé, Micah, was American, and over and over again Alyx emphasised the bureaucratic advantages of them being legally wed. Coronavirus was closing international borders – what if they needed to get between America and Australia? What if decisions were made about borders that prevented them from accompanying each other if they weren't married? What if she couldn't live in Sydney long term because climate change–induced bushfires made it hard for her to breathe every summer with her asthma? What if what if what if?

'When you're talking about a relationship that is not just a relationship between two people, but a relationship between two states, that kind of bureaucratic aspect of marriage becomes completely essential. And because we want to spend the rest of our lives together, we just knew that having this piece of paper that confirms that would make it much easier for us to pass through any bureaucratic hurdles that might come up,' Alyx told me.

Which makes sense, but it is also very ... unromantic. Was it just something she was telling herself? Like how I told myself that I was ambivalent about marriage while still taking part in it? If it really is just a piece of paper, then why not just get the piece of paper? Why bother going through the ritual of a wedding?

Alyx set to work in isolation putting together her outfit (her grandmother's gorgeous wedding-night nightie, which we don't need to think much more about), getting a professional makeup lesson over Zoom and inviting hundreds of their closest friends and family to watch.

After her list of caveats of why she was 'inherently sceptical' about marriage, Alyx told me about what happened after they got engaged that left her 'incredibly shocked'.

'The reaction from other people has been so positive and so emotionally overwhelming in a way ... I know that getting married is a time when your friends come close to you and you get to have the emotional feelings, the conversations that you wouldn't necessarily otherwise engage in because it's difficult or confronting, but this is an allowed space for that – I know all that, but when it happened to me, I was still totally shocked by it, and really in awe of it in a very positive way.

'Our friends threw us a hens' and bucks' party [over Zoom], they made a whole PowerPoint presentation, they went to huge amounts of effort to make us feel special and make the fact that we were doing this feel like a big special occasion. That reinforcement from community and from family, and the idea that a marriage and particularly a wedding is not really about you, it's about everyone in your periphery, has really, really been enforced by this process. It's something that I knew intellectually, and sort of knew emotionally, but it wasn't a truth that I'd necessarily applied to myself ... I kind of had always seen the emotional fallout of weddings and thought, "Seems stressful," but hadn't really metabolised the monumental upsides.'

There are monumental upsides, which a lot of people, people who don't get so 'into their own head' overthinking marriage, see easily. Some people are just happy and know getting married is what happy people do and so they do it. They embrace the hens' party and the props and the styled engagement look and the flowers and the countdown and the dress shopping. It's not exhausting to them, or infused with politics; it's just a good time with someone they love.

There are also lots of us who get into the hens' party and the props and the styled engagement look and the flowers and the countdown and the dress shopping while feeling otherwise, affecting a wry smile all the while. Seemingly incapable of enjoying ourselves or celebrating something as earnest as love without acting like we are being a wee bit ironic.

But. There is always a but. There are reasons to be sceptical. There are reasons to roll your eyes at it. Marriage can be great, but what we're really focused on is the weddings.

The internet has really flattened the aesthetic of weddings. There are a few looks you see over and over again, whether you are looking at photos of a bride in Windsor, England; or New York, USA; or the New South Wales south coast, Australia.

They can be roughly divided into three categories: the country bride, the city bride and the beach bride.

The country bride usually has her hair down in loose waves, can have flowers on her head, and doesn't wear a strapless white dress. Maybe there's lace detailing on the sleeves and maybe she wears shoes that are not high heels. There are fairy lights strung about the reception and food is on big shared boards.

The city bride is thin and wears a tight dress. She usually has her pictures taken against an amazing backdrop, a stunning view across water or a city skyline. She's very slick and very glam. Her reception is in a restaurant and only real champagne is served, with long stick candles on the tables and flowers that cost five figures.

The beach bride can also be a destination bride and leans more into the boho elements the country bride cherry-picks from, walking barefoot with her hair loose and just a lightly stained pink on the lips. Ideally she wants the reception outside where it will definitely be windy, but there is usually a package she can take with a resort in the area she gets married.

It is rare to care about anyone wearing a suit in any of these settings. It doesn't matter if they are a straight or queer couple, there are a very tiny number of suits anyone can get excited about.

As Alyx immediately realised, at its cynical heart, the wedding can be approached as a personal brand-building exercise.

'I have never got more attention. More Instagram likes, more floods of overwhelming positivity from fucking strangers as well as from friends and loved ones, as when we announced our engagement. It was actually quite stressful and overwhelming how intense the first few days after that announcement were,' she said.

'I think, particularly for women, but probably also for men and for gay men, that kind of Instagram wedding moment is something that feels really important and feels like a really big deal.'

What people are really attracted to is not the marriage, but the wedding. I don't care about the relationship of a woman I went to school with 13 years ago. But I want to see her wedding dress from every angle, her hair, what her bridesmaids looked like, how she decorated the reception; I want to look at it all. Even if it looks a lot like the photos I scrolled through last month of the woman I used to sit four desks away from at my first office job.

***

One of the phenomena that typifies our generation is the sheer number of single people. There have never been as many single people in their 30s at any other time in history.

There's a yawning schism between what we are told is OK and the reality of single life. Being single is great for independence if you are financially stable. Being happy in your own company is crucial to being happy in general.

The culture tells us we don't need another person to complete us, but, at the same time, the culture tells us we *definitely* need another person to complete us.

Especially for women, being single can be much better for quality of life and mental health. But factor in house prices or the cost of rent, particularly in cities, and wanting to become a parent at some point and, no matter your gender, race or sexuality, there are a lot of 31-year-olds feeling like their lives are on hold until they are partnered up.

'I'll be able to figure out where to live once I'm in a stable relationship. I'll drink less, I'll be calmer, I'll know what to do on the weekend when I'm in a stable relationship.'

The delay in getting married has even been given a name by researchers – 'waithood' – and has been observed in countries such as Indonesia, America, Singapore, Egypt, Greece, Spain, Iran and France.

The American academic who coined the term, Diane Singerman, has identified four crucial factors in what has been described as an 'epidemic' in marriage delays: a demographic youth bulge, high youth unemployment rates, extraordinarily high wedding costs in a context of low wages, and the resulting delayed sexuality and marriage in societies where marriage signals the entrance into full adulthood (pretty much all societies really).

Waithood isn't necessarily the cause of unhappiness – waithood is partly attributed to people gaining more education and enjoying their 20s before committing – but it can be an unhappy time. A time of feeling like you're in suspended animation, like your life can only get going when factors that are really beyond your control are in place.

The solutions put forward to it by academics are (some would say typically) unhelpful for people who want to get on to the next stage of their life *now*. A *Quartz* article by Cassie Werber, headlined 'Being single in your 30s isn't just bad luck, it's a global phenomenon', notes that in countries as different as Indonesia and the United States of America, it is generally the norm that woman marry men who earn more than them, or at least as much as them, and who have the same level of education as them, if not higher. Werber writes:

> Whether by choice, accident, or a combination of the two, more and more educated and ambitious women are finding themselves unable to find the mate that they want at the time they're searching. It's not for lack of trying. The kind of men they are searching for – available to embark on family life, ready to commit, and with similar levels of education and ambition – simply aren't there in as great numbers as are needed.

Anthropologist Nancy Smith-Hefner has put forward the 'obvious solution' of society accepting the idea of women becoming the major breadwinners for families. Pause for laughter.

So all that 31-year-olds need – from Southeast Asia to western countries – is for society to accept women marrying younger men who are not as educated as them. Or even men of the same age who don't earn as much as them. Great in theory, but what can we do *now* that will actually work?

Ananya is 32 and has already been married for seven years. Her reason was simple: it was time. She is from a big Indian family and there was never any doubt in her mind she would get married and have children. Once she had finished her university degree and was on the career path, marriage was a natural progression for her.

'I think the question is not "Why would I want to get married?", it's "Why wouldn't I get married?" I can't really imagine my life without my community and family, what is more important than that? I have white friends who think that is old-fashioned, but is it? Isn't it the best part of life? Having family and community?'

Ananya said she would never have lived with a man before marriage and she had specific requirements of her husband. So she did what was pragmatic to her and got her parents to find her a man. She wanted someone who spoke her language, was a member of her religion and understood her family, and that's what she got when her parents found Usman for her.

'I have an arranged marriage, which is one of the most shocking things you can say to a lot of people here, but

46

why not? Getting my parents to find my husband I think gave me way better odds of a happy marriage than looking at university or work for a random man,' she said.

Ananya stresses there is a big difference between an arranged marriage and a forced marriage. 'I actually think a lot of my Australian friends should ask their parents to look for a guy. I had a lot of choice in it; my parents put the word out through the community here, in India and the diaspora in places like America and England. They put me in touch with a couple of guys and that pretty quickly fizzled out, and then they found Usman's parents. [Usman and I] just started texting, and then calling, and then visiting each other.'

Within 18 months they were married and now have two daughters. 'I was definitely in love with him when I married him. I have some older relatives who didn't see their husbands until their wedding day – that wasn't like us. We had our common characteristics, but we also had love and it's been wonderful. Marriage is wonderful. It doesn't have to be a burden or a straitjacket. I feel like mine has opened up my life completely.'

***

By the time my best friend, Candice, turned 31, just six months after me, she was already on the other side of millennial marriage – divorce. She had been with her girlfriend for five years when they got married the year they both turned 26. Although it wasn't technically legal yet, they had the wedding and they certainly had the marriage – buying property together and owning cats and a dog, all of which had to be divided in the divorce, which left Candice feeling a lot of guilt. The divorce was complicated by same-sex marriage becoming legal just as she was splitting. She felt like she had let an entire community down.

So why did she get married? Her mother, who is also a lesbian, had never married and didn't expect Candice to, and Candice was one of the first among our mates to do it.

When someone asked Candice this question at the time, she gave a series of bullet points about why marriage was important to her. Afterwards, the person said all they had wanted to hear from Candice was that she was in love.

'At the time, it was definitely because I loved my partner a lot, but I didn't have to get married to prove that,' said Candice. 'I think that getting married as someone in a same-sex relationship at a time when marriage between same-sex partners wasn't legal yet was more important as a statement than it probably should have been. It felt more like I couldn't and should be allowed to do it, so maybe morally I felt the need to prove something … I felt the need to prove my relationship was every bit as real as my married hetero counterparts, and that was a little draining.'

Not only did Candice feel 'imposter-like' about her marriage, she then found herself divorced before 30. An easy divorce is pretty much an oxymoron, but she says she felt there was a lot less stigma than there would have been even 20 years ago.

'It seems like a pretty common divorce reason for a lot of older couples would be infidelity or perhaps even abuse, and while those things definitely still exist, from my experience you can also just not be in love anymore and recognise that long term you'll both be better off if you go through the hard and painful process now,' she said.

'And as for the relationships, I know quite a few divorced couples who at least have an amicable relationship, some who are best friends. It's recognising that you're no longer "that person" for me anymore, but you're still a really important person to me and our relationship can evolve and that's OK!'

Even after having so many complex feelings through her engagement, marriage and divorce, there is still something in getting married that appeals to Candice. It's not as important as it once was, but she can still see herself doing it all over again.

'I think it would have a very different meaning. I think the first time around I felt like it was a lot of doing it for other people, even if I didn't realise at the time, even if it was for people I didn't even particularly care about. But if I did it again, it would have to be 100 per cent for me and my partner,' she said.

***

The kind of bride Alyx turned out to be was ... a beautiful one.

The morning of her wedding, I got up and carefully applied two different shades of gold eyeshadow, did my bronzer in a back-to-front number 3 shape on my face and put on a gold silk dress. Then I sat down at my computer and logged into the video platform she had chosen for her wedding. We could enter different 'sessions', which were like tables, and talk to other guests in there. I saw my friends, with their hair and makeup done, their suits on, just like they would have had we been physically together. The delight was real, as it would have been had we been physically together.

Then we were directed to the 'stage' screen where Micah stood, erect as a biro. He was a little nervous but seemed excited. It must have been eerie to be in a room with just a celebrant and a photographer, but knowing hundreds of other people were watching. Then he started tapping a drum and Alyx appeared, all pale skin and red hair and peach vintage nightie, carrying flowers. Ethereal was the word.

I started to cry. Just like I would have had I been in the room.

I clasped my hands earnestly to my chest during the vows, and cheered and clapped when they kissed. I took a photo of the screen and posted it to Instagram *after* a photo of my own outfit.

I was so happy. I love love. I love watching people in love. I love people celebrating their love. I tend to forget that part when I am thinking about weddings and marriage.

***

I have a line written down in the notes of my phone, and I don't know if I heard someone say it in conversation or on a TV show or in a movie, but it has stuck with me: 'Believe me, choosing to love someone unconditionally, and forgiving them always, no matter how they treat you, and making sure they know it ... that's for Jesus, that ain't for normal people.'

Unconditional love is not a part of marriage. It's not part of most relationships. Of course there are conditions your partner has to meet, even that your parents have to meet – pretty much everyone you love has to meet some basic conditions. Though there are perhaps exceptions to this rule.

Years ago, I was speaking with a very famous English journalist in a pub. He would have been about 60, I was in my mid-20s, and for some reason we started talking about the deaths of his mother and father. What he realised, he told me, was that he was alone in the world. He had a brother, had been married for 35 years and had two adult daughters he was close to, but, he said, there were conditions on their love.

'Of course there are some things I could do that would mean they'd never forgive me,' he said. 'But your mother and father, if you're lucky, you know, you could end up in jail and they would still be around. Mine would've at least. And now I am all alone.'

(I can quote him accurately because I wrote what he said in my diary at the time.)

You have to be just a little bit naïve to get married because of everything that can go wrong after. That my own parents are no longer together has certainly coloured my view of marriage. Mostly the first-hand knowledge that it can end, even when neither person in the relationship is a bad person. That it can be nobody's fault and both of their faults.

My husband's parents have been married for 50 years. Fifty years and they are still so tender and loving towards each other. I don't think I have ever seen them get annoyed with each other, over anything, even those daily things that don't matter that all of us get irritated by, like the tomato sauce being put on the wrong shelf in the fridge.

So when we got married, I did so thinking it might not be forever, and my husband, Matt, did so without it ever occurring to him that it might not be forever, which was extraordinary to me when I realised it. About two and a half years after the wedding, we were having a conversation in which I was insisting we stay together in various hypothetical situations (imagining what I would do in various hypothetical situations is a top-three pastime of mine). 'We're married, why would we break up?' he said to me. It truly shook me that he had taken getting married to mean being together forever. But I guess that's what happens when your parents love each other so much. You believe in it.

Still, the reason we got married was not because he proposed. My mother proposed to me.

I was 26 and visiting home with Matt at the beginning or end of a holiday. It was a hot evening at my mother's house in Grafton and, mortifyingly, it was Valentine's Day.

The evening began with Mum badgering us. 'When are you two going to get married?'

We both shrugged. We probably wouldn't.

'You should get married this year.'

We shrugged again. We probably wouldn't.

But the evening wore on. 'Why don't you get married on my birthday? November 13. That would be nice; it's on a Friday this year. You should get married.'

We shrugged yet again and Matty had another beer and I had another wine.

My mother has never been a big drinker and generally doesn't approve of her children having more than two drinks in a session, but, for some reason, perhaps playing right into her hands, she said nothing as we kept drinking.

Hours later, she was still going. 'Why don't you get married? You should get married. In November!'

We shrugged for the umpteenth time. Matt said, 'OK.'

I turned to him. 'What?'

My mother started jumping up and down.

He turned to me. 'Well, do you want to?'

My mother began yelling, 'You're getting married! You're getting married!'

'OK,' I said. Or words to that effect.

'You're getting married! You're getting married!' My mother was still jumping up and down. And then, in a final genius move, she said to Matt: 'You should call your mother!' My mother is diabolical.

So Matt called his mother, who was thrilled, although puzzled that there was no ring. The phone call made the whole thing real.

The next morning, we realised we couldn't ring Matt's mother back and explain we weren't getting married, we had just been getting harangued by my mother. So we got married. We got married in November of that year, exactly as my mother demanded.

My wedding turned out to be a culmination of years of appeasing my mum. My marriage, though, that's all me and Matt.

We've been in a relationship for 12 years and mostly the cliché of 'marriage being hard work' has not rung true (yet). I think it is hard work to be with me sometimes – I'm not being self-deprecating, or coy, or saying it in that way that means 'Oh, I'm just so complex and *different*.' It's just a fact that I'm a difficult person to be in a relationship with at times. But I don't find it hard work being with Matt. Being with Matt is the easy bit. It's why I don't write about it much; other people's happy relationships are dull.

When I first met Matt, I pursued him so aggressively that I even looked up his favourite books on Myspace and bought them and read them. When he was first in my bedroom, he noticed a copy of one of them and said, 'Oh, I love that book.'

'So do I,' I replied innocently.

And genuinely, *Everything is Illuminated* by Jonathan Safran Foer is still one of my favourite books.

I used every trick I needed to land him, even telling him I was 23 because he was in his early 30s. The look of horror on his face when I revealed I was actually 19 is something I still torture him with.

Being in a long-term relationship, like any worthwhile project, means you have to do it incrementally, day by day, turn up when you say you're going to and be OK with it not playing out the way you thought it would in your head. You have to accept that it's imperfect.

Being happily married seems suburban, a modest goal, but it is a miracle if you can get the alchemy right, easily the best thing in your life that will ever happen to you. If you pull it off.

You can have all these things without getting married; you can turn up day after day for your partner without the party. But marriage is not an empty institution. Millennials still get married because, even though it is old-fashioned, and can seem naff, it is a supreme act of optimism. And finding real love is something worth celebrating. The big, consuming love: it's the best. You are going to have a party for graduating university? For a promotion? Why not have a party for something that really matters – being in love!

We are getting married because there is a massive industry built around weddings that encourages us to do so, we are getting married because it is an exercise in self-branding, we are getting married because our parents did, we are getting married because we want to do better than our parents did, we are getting married because we are in love and we are getting married because we love a party.

We are getting married because it is a time when we are a bit starved of supreme acts of optimism.

Grief and malaise

Unhappiness as you hit 31 has many facets. There is a bitterness to it. Even reading that could make you baulk, let alone admitting it to yourself. It is ugly to be bitter – uglier still to recognise bitterness within yourself – but it is something quite settled in many of us.

Being sour is usually associated with older people, women in particular, but like the more general misery, it is not gendered for millennials. It can be lazy to generalise, but a phenomenon I have noticed among my friends, online and within myself is a smug satisfaction when declaring certain traits, such as existential dread and a tendency for self-annihilation. It's usually a particular type of formerly precocious 30-something-year-old who references them, someone whose life has not lived up to expectations despite their talent in whatever field.

Nobody has an air of self-satisfaction when owning up to misery. There is a hard edge to the misery; a self-indulgence to the bitterness. Twinned with it is jealousy. Envy of your peers is a phenomenon as ancient as the concept of friends, but combined with bitterness it has fermented into a type of grief. A grief that we missed out on reaping what our usually advantageous positions might otherwise have sowed. People feel ripped off. It used to be that if you were born or made it into the middle class, you got property; now you don't even get financial stability. You used to be able to wring a living out of various creative endeavours; now to be a writer or a painter or a performer in Australia, you either have to have two or three other jobs, or you have to come from the upper class.

Fairly recently, there was a simple career trajectory if you managed to get a full-time job, each year your wages would rise, small businesses thrived, and there were more options outside of major cities. Now inequality grows; outside of the public service, job stability is rarer; and wages have stagnated for more than a decade.

***

When my aunt Veronica died, a few months before I turned 30, it was an agony. She died at home, with people who loved her so much: her three sons, her husband, her brother, her sister. But she was too young. She wasn't even 60, she had a lot of good years left. At least she was at home, though; at least she wasn't alone. That's what we kept telling ourselves at the time.

You're supposed to be grateful even when everything is so shit.

That morning, my brother and sisters and I went to the pier with her sons, all in their early 20s. In their early 20s and their mum was dead. It was unfathomable to me. Still is.

The weather was mocking us that day, the sky stunning with picturesque streaks of clouds, the ocean sparkling and calm. We walked past an older couple, who greeted us, openly commenting what a beautiful day it was. How were they supposed to know we were with three young men who would never be the same again? A curious part of that kind of grief, which everyone experiences at some point, is witnessing people behave as if it's a normal day. You saw your mother dead in the living room that morning. A couple still takes a pleasant stroll along the pier. It's a bucket of cold water over your head.

Journalist David Marr wrote about walking outside the hospital after his father died: 'There was a woman rushing down the hill to the station. I wanted to yell: It doesn't matter!' That is exactly how it feels.

The boys did not speak to the couple, but I said hello to them. There was nothing else I could do for my cousins but excuse them from social niceties. In the hierarchy of grief, theirs mattered more than mine, of course. It would have been petulant and melodramatic for me to ignore the real world carrying on.

'It's not fair,' I thought. And then: 'What a staggeringly unoriginal thought.'

It was and is not fair that Veronica was dead and someone like the Queen gets to live into her 90s.

But there is plenty in the world that is a lot more unjust. It's not fair that an accident of birth means it is not a financial burden for me to pay back the cost of my university degree, and I could go my entire life not paying it back with no penalty, while my Nepal-born babysitter has to save tens of thousands of dollars a year with her cleaner husband so she can become a nurse in Australia. A job we actually need while I faff about with words. People just two generations ahead of me did not have to pay at all for the degrees that made them lawyers and doctors and public servants. If education is the great equaliser, we have only submitted more and more to the gatekeeping of its opportunity.

My babysitter has real reason to be bitter and she is not; I have less reason and I am a bit. It's juvenile to cling to any expectation of fairness in life, especially when there is so much already weighted in my favour. But it's also important to cling to a notion of fairness in life, otherwise it's too easy to let other people suffer as long as you aren't.

Still, my petulance could not be helped that October morning. We don't have to be too upstanding in our grief.

I often thought of that morning during a terrified March and April in 2020. How a private, personal thing such as grief can suddenly be collective. How a lot of 31-year-olds already had been doing a collective bereavement, although not as publicly.

As more than half a million people lost their jobs within a month in Australia, and as we watched the death toll climb in Italy and then New York, it was weeks of pure terror. It's easy to forget how scared we were. Everyone was confused, everyone was afraid. Unless you were a rabid consumer of the news who had foreseen the eventual lockdown or are someone who always expects the worst-case scenario, it was a shock to suddenly be stuck in your home. I was a news journalist and *I* was shocked to be shut in my home. It happened so quickly that the last time I caught the train home from work in 2020, one afternoon in March, I had left an orange on my office desk along with my personal photos.

I still don't know how that orange is doing.

On a Friday in March, our prime minister said that he was still going to the footy on the weekend. Then suddenly we were told to stop seeing our friends and family and only leave our homes when essential. The hospitality industry crumbled within days, planes were grounded, the weekend footy stopped. This didn't happen over the course of months or even weeks. It happened within days. We were in shock together, and then we were grieving our old lives together. There is an element of human connection we get with this kind of solidarity of experience that is the precise opposite of the abandonment we feel in personal grief.

When I left my house, it wasn't in a bubble of my own agony. I wasn't the only one scared I wouldn't be able to pay the rent in a couple of months. I wasn't the only one scared about my parents suddenly dropping dead. I wasn't part of a tiny cohort whose entire world had shifted on its axis, like when Veronica died. There was no looking at other people thinking, 'I can't believe you get to get on with your normal life.' Instead we looked at each uneasily across apples in the supermarket, standing 1.5 metres apart, both thinking something like, 'I can't believe we don't have a normal life anymore.'

The ease with which we slipped into nostalgia was comical.

'Remember RSVPing yes to parties you had no intention of going to?' we said to each other wistfully over Zoom.

'Remember how crowded the train was on a Monday morning?'

'Remember braiding your friend's hair?'

'Remember breakfast buffets?'

This came naturally to millennials because we had been practising this collective delusion of nostalgia for a couple of years already. It was part of the malaise we moved into in our early 30s. The feeling – we were convinced it was the *knowledge* – that things had been better. Not only in our early 20s, although we acted as if we were the first to be nostalgic for the freedom and ignorance of then; we also had nostalgia for the early 30s of Gen Xers and boomers, whose lives in general worked out very differently at the same stage.

'Imagine being able to buy an actual house in your 20s,' we would say to each other.

'When my mother was my age, she had three children!'

'Imagine having one job you clock out of at 5 pm each day.'

Things had been better and now they are only getting worse. And worse. And worse. We wailed for a naive bliss that we thought we once had in our 20s, but we also wailed for the lives we felt we were robbed of, that people before us got.

Then coronavirus hit and we grieved what up until then had been the lopsided compensations of being robbed of security – nobody had ever travelled so widely and so cheaply en masse as us at the same age. It was socially acceptable for us to party and hug our sweaty mates in our early 30s unlike a couple of decades before. We were more emotionally open with those we love after doing away with 'appearances'. But within a few days, travel as we knew it ended, we were banned from seeing our friends unless it was over an annoying video-conferencing site or platform, and nobody knew when we would ever be allowed in a crowd of sweaty strangers again, waiting for the cap to hit while the bass was rising. Our prospects had dwindled long ago and now our lives were tiny too. The lockdown was not unique to any generation, but it was difficult to not feel cheated. To not be bitter.

If we were lucky, the social constraints were our primary concern.

I am fond of saying some people have real problems, without anyone ever making me define what a 'real problem' is. Someone expressing their unhappiness can be characterised as having 'first-world problems'. Often the poor are used as an example of being much worse off, which they are, but they are held up as if they are too virtuous to fret about how their lives are turning out, what they have missed out on, not being able to see their mates.

***

Of course, there are people who are not grieving something as abstract as the life they could have had. Even mourning the life you actually used to have is still not grieving a person. A real person you will never see again.

For some millennials, grief like that has already been confronted, is already being carried into their age of malaise with everyone else. This grief for millennials at its basics looks much the same as it has for everyone for centuries – devastating, surreal, and not as unique as the person in the midst of it thinks.

As author Martin Amis said, 'Nobody is spared the main events', but they do come earlier for some of us than others.

Que Minh Luu saw similarities between the collective grief we went through in 2020 and the grief of watching someone she loved die, although hers was much more acute than mine for aunt Veronica (grief isn't a competition, but she definitely beat me).

Que's partner and father of her child, Jesse, died in December 2017 when he was just 31. Que wrote that she had to relearn how to live.

Her grief did not begin when he died, though; it began when he was diagnosed with a rare soft tissue cancer and life as they knew it was suddenly taken from them.

'That destabilising feeling of the ground giving way under our feet feels familiar to me. This time though, we're all simultaneously in our own centres of grief, clinging to routine, safety and connection, even as we grapple with the fear and loss,' she wrote for the *Guardian*. 'What is such an anxious, unmooring and devastating time for so many means a blind grab onto what's left that is normal.'

After spending years being nostalgic for someone else's youth – the ease of life for adults in the 1980s, for example – we were suddenly nostalgic for what we had been able to do months before. In my blind grab on to what was left that was normal, I promised I would never again take for granted:

- My parents' health
- My parents
- Having a choice to stay in or go out
- Walking into a pub
- Apologising after accidentally elbowing a stranger because we were standing so close together
- Sharing a cigarette (even though I should never have another cigarette)
- Going out spontaneously
- Doing anything spontaneously.

Isn't this the resolution you make every time you find yourself unable to take part in simple pleasures? Every time you hear a shocking story of someone else's misfortune? 'I will never again take things for granted.' Lying in KFC-stained sheets, vomiting from the eighth lurid cocktail the night before, you think, 'I am never drinking that much again.' Recovering from a particularly bad illness, you stare out the window and think, 'I will never take being able to walk outside easily for granted again.' Down the burning east coast of Australia during the 2019/2020 summer a lot of us thought, 'I will never take clean air for granted again.'

There is a bit of a self-improvement bent to it. Our compulsion to tell ourselves we can do and be better, that we have been doing it wrong.

But we do take these things for granted again. We will.

We recover, we get caught up in the fun of another night out, the memory of that summer of bushfires is surpassed by something else.

Lockdown reminded me of my first pregnancy, the suspended animation of waiting, of not being able to make simple decisions and do simple things. I know so many people who were shocked by the reality of pregnancy. Something we think of as so unremarkable – our mothers did it! How hard can it be! – actually takes a massive toll on our bodies; it can be very painful, debilitating, restrictive. I can tell you about how psychologically difficult it can be, how worn down you are at the end by sickness and fatigue, how you can't do anything that you previously didn't think twice about – walking up a hill, changing positions in your sleep, breathing easily. I can tell you how hard it is, but I can't explain it. Then you have to go through childbirth, the closest description of which I've heard is from my friend who said it 'is like dying, like walking through fire'.

During my first pregnancy, every time I went to the pub I mourned the good time I could have been having as I watched people order a second, third, fourth, even fifth drink without a second thought. I would turn away from the fun to go home because I just couldn't keep my eyes open. I couldn't choose what I wanted to wear; instead, it was dictated each day by how my body had changed. I couldn't even wear my shoes because my feet went up a size. Once I was visibly pregnant, people who did not know me, and even those who did, felt they could tell me what was best for me, like how many cups of coffee I should or should not drink.

It sounds silly, but it's not. When every small act of independence is taken away, it adds up.

Lockdown reminded me a lot of my first pregnancy in that we were all very focused on what we had lost and were in denial about how much was changing.

That's the millennial condition in a simple sentence: very focused on what we have lost and in denial about how much is changing.

If things seem difficult, it's because they *are* difficult, but there is also so much to celebrate. Can I labour (haha) the metaphor of my first pregnancy into life after recession and in our 30s? What came after that horrible pregnancy was joy so much beyond my very limited imagination. We are not going to get a lot of the opportunities for stability that previous generations did, but there will still be opportunities, hopefully for a wider variety of people.

Yes, houses were cheaper in the 1980s, but I would not have wanted to be a woman in many workplaces in the 1980s. Unless maybe I was Tina Brown being made the editor of *Vanity Fair* in New York at the age of 30. Yes, the middle class has drastically shrunk, but that was a middle class overwhelmingly made up of white people – maybe now there is a chance for more diverse, more equal prosperity.

There could be a chance at building something that is better than was before.

Our lives are not turning out the way we thought they would. Well, maybe yours is. *My* life is not turning out the way I thought it would. There are petty jealousies, thwarted ambitions, depressing financial realities, signs of ageing that, frankly, seem shocking and outrageous to me. There is a semblance of control that is constantly slipping away.

But this grief at what is gone, and nostalgia for what other people have and I will never have a chance at, this grief and nostalgia does not have to be the end of something. It can be used to create something that is different. It can be used for something more exciting. It also may be misplaced. Do we really have it that much harder than the generations before us?

The thing about nostalgia is that it's a trick. It's you missing something that is not real, missing the way you thought something *should* have been, not the way it actually was. Nostalgia makes anything difficult a mere punctuation mark in a more glorious story. You forget what was painful or hard or boring about something, see it as you wish it was. It tricks you into being bitter about something that wasn't even true.

I like being addicted to my phone

Sometimes I imagine my children's children's children scrolling through my Instagram, an archive of their great-grandmother in her prime.

'She thought she was funny,' they will say, and it will be an accurate insight into their great-grandmother at 31. I do think I am funny!

'Ugh, why did they post photos of books they read back then?' one will ask. 'They thought it made them look cleverer than they actually were,' another will reply. And they will also be right.

I think about this scenario, not only because I have a tendency for self-indulgence (duh), but also because if a stranger – even a stranger who loved me in some abstract way, such as a great-grandchild who perhaps had never met me – were to look at my Instagram feed, they would definitely be able to glean some things about me. It would be nothing like meeting me – there is no substitute for meeting me – but they would be able to tell some things about me. And it is fun to look at your social media feeds as if you are a stranger and try to guess what people would think.

There is a photo that exists in my family that Mum and I have visceral reactions to. It is of me, my brother, my sisters, both of my parents, Matt and one of my best friends, Rick. All the kids are in our 20s and are standing in what looks to be a field with bush in the background. My youngest sister, Alice, is taking the photo as a selfie, sunglasses on, cap on backwards, her mouth open in an exaggerated smile. The photo is framed so Matt, Mum, Dad, Rick, my brother Séamus and my other sister Anna are posing in the background, crowded together with their arms around each other. I stand slightly apart, staring at the camera, unable to smile.

At this point in time, my parents aren't together but have been friends with each other for years and there is genuinely no tension between them. It looks like a pretty nice photo of a rare reunion between the six adult members of an immediate family. And Rick. Me standing apart could have been a fluke of the photo; I could have just been unprepared.

Before this photo was taken, I had just given my sisters a six-hour lift in my car and arrived at my parents in tears. I hadn't seen my sisters in months. They had both lost a lot of weight, and I didn't like the people they were living with. I was almost hysterical with concern when I saw my mother. My sisters were acting like everything was fine. Alice asked us to pose for the photo, so we did, but whenever Mum looks at it she can only see how distressed I am and I can only see the dread I was filled with.

It's a nice photo. It could even be a funny photo because I look so cranky while everyone else is smiling.

I assume almost every person has a photo of themselves like this. Looks great, but, far out, what a terrible time we were having in reality. This is normal. It should be pretty normal, then, for most people to look at photos of other people and assume it is not telling them everything.

It is fashionable to lament the hold of the smartphone on our lives, by which most people mean social media. Stanford professor Jenny Odell wrote a 10,000-word talk, which went viral after she posted it online, on the 'importance of doing nothing'. Eighteen months later, she had expanded the talk into a *New York Times* bestselling book. Odell made completely fair points about the need for public space and how good it is for the mind to get into nature and away from the computer. But there was a delicious irony in someone with her resume (teacher at Stanford University, exhibiting artist, published writer) turning her 'doing nothing' into a bestselling book, which characterised some parts of the internet as driving our need to monetise all of the 24 hours in a day and distracting us from what is important.

She also describes herself as a 'lover of weird internet things', but a big part of her solution to modern malaise is stepping away from it.

There is obviously an appetite for what could be categorised as 'things that will make us feel better', but hasn't there always been? For many centuries before the internet?

Kevin Roose, a technology columnist at the *New York Times*, even characterised reducing his phone use as 'unbreaking' his brain. This kind of discourse is usually tied up in talk about how 'the internet is not real life' and how young people (although they can mean anyone from 13-year-olds to millennials, who started turning 40 in 2020) seem to be too distracted by it.

I don't think young(ish) people are that confused by what they see on the internet, and I also think there is a lot of real life on there. Who is populating these social media feeds, if not real people? (OK, there may also be a Russian bot or two.) Doesn't that make it real?

'Is the internet real?' could be the longest op-ed in the history of newspapers, locked by moderators after 3,498 pages of uncivil discourse.

'Instagram isn't real' is a common catch-cry, but it is real. I really did go to that café, I was really in Paris when that photo was taken, and I really do more or less look like that when I am dressed up and get my makeup professionally done. I think it's too simple to claim people think that my trip to Paris was perfect and I always look like that. People aren't idiots – when they post their own version of their lives on social media, they know it isn't telling the full story.

Posting only about what is fun and interesting to you can be perceived as dishonesty, but that isn't the only place dishonesty exists. Most of us don't go to work on Monday and tell our colleagues about the fight we had with our girlfriend, or that we couldn't get out of bed until 2 pm, or even that we found ourselves kind of lonely on Saturday night. We are actually more likely to say those things on a Reddit thread, but the point is there is a version of ourselves that we present on Monday morning, just like there is a version of what happened that we tell on social media.

We have become so aware of this curation that a new trend was spawned pretty quickly on social media – that of the 'being real' post. Tavi Gevinson was an influencer before we even had a word for influencers, before Instagram even existed. She was propelled to fashion celebrity when she was just 12 years old after starting the blog Style Rookie. There are photos of her, slight and still very childlike after she officially became a teenager at 13, with Anna Wintour in New York during fashion week. She was a regular at fashion shows before she was even halfway through puberty. A gifted writer, she left the blog behind to launch an online magazine, eventually moving to New York to become an actor and garnering 500,000 Instagram followers along the way. An extraordinary amount of success for any age, let alone in the decade before hitting her early 20s.

In 2019 she wrote a front-page essay for *The Cut* on how the life she portrayed on Instagram was not like her real life.

'Somewhere along the line, I think I came to see my shareable self as the authentic one and buried any tendencies that might threaten her likability so deep down I forgot they even existed,' she said.

But it is not Instagram's fault she didn't want to think about the parts of herself that she didn't like; that is a perfectly natural impulse. There are not many of us, especially when we are in our early 20s, who spend a lot of time on any real self-examination. Who can openly acknowledge our faults and basest ambitions.

And even fewer of us who acknowledge how mundane those base ambitions really are: to be admired, to be liked, to be thought of as clever and, as a bonus, attractive. Even when we know we are really not that clever.

Mostly this is enacted on the internet through social media. The easiest place to get immediate feedback on your looks, wit and life is on one of the big platforms: Facebook, Instagram, Twitter, and more recently TikTok. People have different motivations for logging on. Some people want to keep in touch with old friends and relatives; some people want to shake out their feelings on the news of the day, be part of the conversation, even if it's only with pithy remarks; and some people want to give an impression to people of the life they are living. At the core of any of these reasons is a kind of longing – 'I'm here! See me!' – which underpins all social media.

Tavi has had the feedback of thousands of people, maybe even more, since she was very young, so she does articulate an experience with the internet that truly shaped her, but she also writes about things people have been grappling with long before we even had landlines.

'After countless adventures through the black hole, my propensity to share, perform, and entertain has melded with a desire far more cynical: to be liked, quantifiably, for an idealized version of myself, at a rate not possible even ten years ago,' she wrote.

It was a fine piece, but surely we already knew most of it. Why was it shared so widely then? It feeds into the insecurities we are told we have because of Instagram, but which would likely still exist without it. Insecurity about our place in the world; insecurity about the way we look; insecurity about whether people are having more fun than us, more fulfilling experiences; insecurity about, well, everything.

There can't be that many people left taking everything they see at face value, or that many people who don't want to be an idealised version of themselves anyway.

When researchers from King's College London released a review of 41 studies into phone use, it was dutifully covered with headlines such as 'One in four teenagers "face mental health risk" from phone addiction'.

News outlets love a headline about people being addicted to their phones, particularly teenagers. The most common criteria for assessing overuse of a phone include being on it for longer than they had intended, whether it had caused them to miss some planned schoolwork, or if they had been told by others they were using it too much.

I can answer yes to all of the above for my phone, for books, for television, for being at the pub and for basically anything enjoyable in life.

If those are the parameters for addiction, I quite like being addicted to my phone. My phone is pretty interesting.

Without it, I wouldn't be as widely read as I am. I wouldn't have learned about the terrible phenomenon of parents accidentally leaving their children in cars to die or know how to make the most delicious spinach pie in 30 minutes. I wouldn't know what market socialism is, I wouldn't have learned about the Bosnian war and I wouldn't have my job, since I found the job advertisement that got me where I am today while idly scrolling Twitter. I would have a completely different circle of friends (maybe better actually, who knows) and I wouldn't talk to some of my cousins on the other side of the world as frequently as I do. I would have felt a lot more isolated during the 2 am feeds with a tiny newborn, but I would probably also have written this book a lot faster.

All of the above is thanks to a mish-mash of apps on my phone: calling apps, which make it free or at least a lot cheaper to talk to people internationally; social media apps; and browsers where I can deep-dive into good old-fashioned rabbit holes of information that start on Wikipedia, take me through to news articles from 1987 and end on old forums as I keep googling, keep clicking through.

I have to be at home from 7 pm pretty much every night of the working week, because I am keeping another human alive and my husband works evenings, and those nights would be a hell of a lot more boring without my phone. Perhaps my house would be cleaner, though.

When people imagine what they would do if they weren't mindlessly scrolling, they think of grand things: 'I could be writing a novel, or at least reading a novel.' But it's the same illusion that people with small children have about what they would do with all their free time if they didn't have kids. They think of being able to go off on holiday at a whim and reading books (reading more books features fairly heavily in people's idea of their imaginary selves), when actually you would probably just do what you did before you had kids. Get accidentally drunk on a Wednesday night more frequently and watch a lot of television.

It's the same with phones. If you didn't have a phone, you would have a much better attention span, but you would also get lost a lot more frequently and you wouldn't be able to track exactly how far away the train is.

I don't want to be too blasé – there are legitimate concerns about phone use, particularly with children. We even have new terminology related to pathological phone use such as nomophobia, the fear of going without your phone; textaphrenia, the fear that you can't send or receive texts; and, one we have likely all experienced, phantom vibrations, which is the feeling that your phone is alerting you when it really isn't.

The journal *JAMA Pediatrics* published a study linking screen time at two and three years old with slower development at five years old. Those who spent more time on screens at earlier ages performed worse later on development tests such as drawing shapes, copying certain behaviours and speaking in sentences.

'When young children are observing screens, they may be missing important opportunities to practice and master interpersonal, motor, and communication skills,' the authors wrote.

Like a lot of suboptimal behaviour, research shows phone use tends to peak in teen years and decline after. A review of research in *Frontiers of Psychology* found that problematic phone use was linked with low self-esteem, low impulse control, anxiety, depression and, weirdly, being highly extroverted.

However, and there is a however.

Researchers responding to the study on children said screen time did not have as much of an impact as sleep, socioeconomic background and whether the child was read to.

The authors of the *Frontiers of Psychology* analysis did not find that phone use was the cause of these linked issues, or whether the problematic phone use happened *because* people were anxious or depressed or, weirdly, highly extroverted. Which comes first, the phone use or the anxiety? We simply don't know, but phones are an easy scapegoat for society's ills.

What hasn't been studied properly is the difference between spending time on your phone messaging friends or reading, and spending time on your phone watching endless YouTube videos. Even Jean Twenge, a professor of psychology at San Diego State University, told the *Verge*: 'that would be a great study. I hope it's done.' The reason it hasn't been done is that most studies focus solely on screen time and rely on self-reporting of hours spent on the phone, rather than what is actually being done on the phone. Phone use and phone psychology is still a fairly new field.

I wouldn't be so arrogant to say that there is no negative impact of phone use, but I think there is certainly a moral panic that at best has overblown the effects and at worst clouded the actual research. The University College London experts who led a study on screen time that found social media had a detrimental effect on young people were reluctant to issue guidelines on how much time teens should spend online. Setting daily limits, they say, is 'not the right focus'. Instead, parents should be thinking: 'Are you getting enough sleep, enough exercise, are you spending enough time with your family?' Research from Oxford University has even found correlation between about two hours of screen time a day and greater physical, social and emotional wellbeing.

What I don't doubt is that phones have changed our behaviour. I know the way I think is deeply influenced by the internet. Writing this chapter, I am also thinking about tweeting, 'I am working on my magnum opus: screens are hell good, actually.' This is how I think a lot of the time. In 200-character-ish one-liners. Pithy, self-deprecating, cool. Thinking about posting even while trying to write a 4000-word essay. My brain is being rewired, but is it worse than the way it was wired before? What could I be thinking about instead? The task at hand, sure, but I would think even Shakespeare was not solely focused on the creative task at hand at all times. He could have also thought about whether a break at the pub might help to clear a spell of writers' block, whether it was more pressing to eat some pear pie than write – any excuse not to do the actual work. The compulsion to do something else other than write must have always been there, it's just become easier to satisfy.

Flicking across various news, social media and even banking apps at 9 pm has become just another thing to feel guilty about in a long, long list.

Here is a stern warning issued by the ABC about over-listening to the radio many decades ago:

> No one, however leisured his or her life, ought to listen all the time. There would be something excessive and intemperate about such a person. Yet, like so many other things, listening to wireless transmissions may become a habit, and a bad habit. Fear that one may be missing something by not listening is one cause; but a more insidious one is the feeling that something is going on somewhere, and that rather than take the trouble to do anything for oneself, one might as well listen to it. That, of course, is as great an injustice to the art of Broadcasting as it is to the listener himself. It is a misuse of what, properly used, can be a very real boon to the aesthetic life of any household.

It's becoming a tired point, but there were similar panics about television and every technological advancement in the past 200 years. The phone is here to stay, and I don't think it has made a significant number of people's lives measurably worse.

If the smartphone, and probably the internet in general, has taken much from me – my time, my ability to concentrate, and my self-esteem on occasion – it is my earnestness that I most care about. I know I used to unself-consciously care about a lot more things. I could find a particular passage so beautiful I would cry, a politician would inspire proper hope in me, I would get very excited about the release of a new book by a mainstream writer. But social media has helped turn a lot of things into a joke. It's not exactly that it is cool not to care (although it is cool not to care); it is that everything has a punchline.

Everything seems ironic, and nothing sacred. It is best summed up in a tweet from Darren Rovell, a sports business reporter and producer, in 2016 as Donald Trump was confirmed as the Republican candidate for president of the United States of America: 'I feel bad for my country, but this is tremendous content.'

My sense is that the ironic voice of the internet is a haphazard, conflicted acknowledgement. That, by being on Twitter, we're all generating content and wealth for an ethically unsound company. This has helped develop the 'too-cool-for-school' deflection of seeming not to care. Tragedies have never been more real – we have never been able to get such up-to-date information so quickly, or footage from so many points of view. Mass outpourings of grief are not uncommon on social media, but they are over as quickly as they begin. In the past, the sanctity and solemnity of mass death was to some degree dealt with by ritual, and the rituals of social media are absolutely terrible for that.

A battery of information every day has helped desensitise me, that much is certainly true. But without the internet, I might not even know half of the awful realities that I should be aware of as a privileged citizen who can help with my money or my voice.

The preoccupation with authenticity is the flipside of irony-soaked social media, but the preoccupation seems to begin and end with how people think they are being perceived on the internet.

Is anyone honest on the internet? Do we have to be? Well, I think the more pertinent question is, is anyone honest with themselves?

Sure, it's flippant, but it's also true (the Bridie Jabour motto).

Authenticity is invoked as much as capitalism is online, by people who could be making a good point but actually only vaguely know what they are talking about. Are you going to watch this sunset because your authentic self wants to or are you going to watch it so you can post a photograph of it? Who cares, if you are still seeing the sunset either way?

Our online selves are, after all, not created in a vacuum; there are elements of our real personalities, our real tastes, our real thoughts online. It's nice to rack up the likes and retweets, but we have been seeking other people's approval for centuries – society is built on caring what other people think.

The internet is real because it is populated by these real people.

Some of the concerns around it are very bourgeois – but I enjoy having bourgeois concerns because they are mostly to do with how we live, manners, travel and other things that make life enjoyable.

This isn't to say my encounters with harassment online have been nothing. I was 25 when I first started to appear on television and the reaction was fierce. I have been threatened with rape more times than I can count, once for making a mild comment about a budgetary measure worth just a few million.

I have been called ugly, stupid, disgusting; told to die; had photos of my baby son posted online with comments about his supposed deficiencies thanks to me; had videos made about me. Even my sister, a teenager at the time, was tracked down and told that she should be raped with a whiskey bottle – for being my sister.

It is nowhere near as bad as it used to be, but for a couple of years, whenever I went on television, I had to turn my phone off afterwards, such would be the bile directed towards me.

I don't accept that this should be the price of being a woman who is sometimes on television, and I certainly don't accept that it is the price women should pay for being online. But it does not make the internet an unequivocally bad place. There are great swathes of society that could have destroyed my sense of worth before the internet could.

For people of colour, queer people, and others who don't happen to look as average as me, the abuse is much, much worse. But for a lot of people who cannot afford to have bourgeois concerns all the time, the internet has radically advanced their fight.

One of the most widely cited examples is the spotlight on police brutality in the USA. Police have been assaulting and shooting Black people in the USA for years, but it has only come to national and international significance with the rise of Black Lives Matter, a movement with extraordinary online recognition. As writer and lawyer Nyadol Nyuon pointed out in a piece for the *Guardian*, at least Twitter is a platform for the 'preferably unheard', even if there are trolls on there. 'It is not established that the traditional media provides a more civil debate than Twitter,' she wrote.

'Implicit in ongoing debate about the incivility of social media is the assumption that traditional media does a better job of fostering civilised debate. There are reasons which make it hard to readily accept that conclusion.'

Black people are not the only marginalised group to benefit from the internet. It's also where trans people have been able to build a platform, and where fat people could look at beautiful photos of other fat people after being all but erased from the mainstream media.

Jonno Revanche has written in the *Guardian* about how much Tumblr helped them when they were growing up queer and isolated in Adelaide.

'When I was uncertain about my latent queerness and gender identity, witnessing other young people navigate those same issues in an open, honest way was incredibly validating for me. They proved that there could be more layers to those things than the stereotypes I saw portrayed in the culture at large,' they said.

***

If my addiction to my phone seems more like an addiction to the internet, or specifically social media, that's because it encompasses all these things. And that's before I even figure out how much time I spend in my group chats. It's why the term 'phone addiction' is pretty much meaningless, and that does not bode well for the studies and news articles on 'phone addiction'. What are we talking about when we talk about 'phone addiction'? Hours spent on YouTube? Wikipedia? Reddit? Dailymail.co.uk? Random academic PDFs published in 1993? Social media? Messaging apps? The compulsion to refresh your bank balance over and over to see if it has changed? It's all on your phone.

My personal phone addiction is made up of Instagram, Twitter, iMessage, Pocket and four news sites. It's why my phone addiction is so wrapped up with my sense of self, because a lot of it is about how I mediate myself online. Screen time does include a lot of social media use for me, but it's used interchangeably by a lot of academics, journalists and civilians.

***

I have spent a lot of time on Instagram insisting other people see me for the person I want to be. I don't think many people are fooled by it. Knowing who you are is not as easy as deactivating your Instagram or refusing to engage with social media. It's tough work.

When I flick through Instagram imagining I am my great-grandchildren, imagining I am in my early 20s looking at what is ahead of me, it is hard to tell what I see.

Someone who is trying hard, probably, even though we are not meant to try hard and we are certainly not meant to *look* like we are trying hard.

Just as Instagram has flattened an aesthetic so a marble coffee table and gold-trimmed lamps next to a leather couch with pale-pink cushions could be in Bali or Los Angeles or Sydney, social media has also flattened the discourse. There is a certain flippant way of speaking online – 'this seems normal' – that has also bled into the views that people hold.

Slowly I have stopped making fun of so much stuff on Twitter, not because it is easy to criticise (it really is, though), but because I have realised I will become what

I now find easy to mock. I will be moved by something (or most likely someone) others deem unworthy; I will think the wrong political party has done a good thing; I'll like the wrong book, song, movie. I am not very good at maintaining a cool detachment from ... anything. If being in my 30s has brought any wisdom, it is that I will at some point be someone who a younger version of myself thought was lame. I will certainly not be seen as cool by any of my great-grandchildren.

Reasons not to have children

When Laura was 31, she decided she wanted a new car. A cool car. A sporty little two-door car. She had been driving an SUV for a few years and had grown tired of it. She didn't need the four doors and the big boot.

She knew what car she wanted and went into her local dealership to ask if they could get it in for her. Up until that point, it all seemed very straightforward. A boring story about a 30-something-year-old in north Queensland buying a car.

'Being Townsville, they said, "Oh no, we can't do that, most women your age go the other way, they trade for the family car." And I said, "Oh yeah, that's just not where I am at," and they deadset, seriously, tried to sell me a Toyota Aurion,' she says.

'I told them, "I really don't think you are understanding me as a potential customer." But they wouldn't do it. I actually went online and purchased the car down in

Melbourne. Did the whole transaction online, flew down, picked it up, drove it home myself.'

Laura had to drive her cool new car for 27-ish hours because people at a dealership could not believe a woman in her early 30s had decided she did not want children.

When she was growing up, Laura vaguely thought she would have children one day, but, as she progressed through her 20s, she thought maybe she would just have one. Then slowly she realised she didn't want one, she wanted none. She got married in her late 20s to a partner who felt the same way, and was very open to her family and friends about not wanting children, but she says it was not until she traded in the SUV for the sports car that a lot of them finally accepted it.

'I posted photos of it online and said, "How cool, I got a new car," and that was what was the nail in the coffin for people who may have been holding out hope that kids might be on the horizon. But they just definitely weren't for us,' she says.

***

One of the biggest decisions a 31-year-old will make is whether to have a child or not. It is one of those decisions where it really matters if you decide to do it and it really matters if you decide not to do it. You can't just skate past it. But not having a child seems a much more active choice than having a child. People don't usually ask you why you decided to have children. When I do ask people that question, they can be surprisingly vague. 'Oh, it was just time,' I hear over and over again.

Despite the availability of contraception and (slightly) increased access to abortion, before the global health pandemic, it did not seem like millennials were more or less likely than previous generations to decide not to have children. The realities of climate change have never been more stark, we are less financially secure, the possibilities of what to do with our lives have expanded, yet since 1976 the proportion of the population who do not have children has oscillated between 21 and 24 per cent, according to Dr Bronwyn Harman, who is studying attitudes towards child freedom in Australia at Edith Cowan University.

So how do you decide not to have a child? When I asked Laura what made her decide, she laughed.

'I just don't want to. It sounds silly but I don't feel like I need a child for me to be complete as a functioning member of our society. I'm happy with who I am, I just don't want to.'

If I had preconceived notions about why people decided not to have children, they were that people were concerned about the environment, they didn't want to lose their freedom, or they couldn't afford it. Of course I came across these reasons, but the overwhelming response echoed Laura's: 'I just don't want to.'

Dr Harman's research backs this up. She agrees the number-one reason is a lack of maternal or paternal instinct. I suspect there are a lot of parents who also do not possess the instinct. It's so easy to do what is expected of you and what is expected of you is to have children. This expectation is everywhere you look, from your own parents (mostly) to the focus of government budgets (with good economic and social reasons) and well-meaning questions from friends.

There is also the small biological imperative in having children: if people did not procreate, we would die out as a species. But at the moment there are more than enough people on the planet, and it's never been easier to not have children. So it's kind of amazing how many people keep doing it.

'In Tasmania [where Laura is originally from], and here locally, people my age, it's what they do. And the scary thing is, now a lot of those people who I went to school with, they've got children, some of them are in primary school and some of them are even in high school, [and the parents themselves,] they're going through either marriage trouble, they're going through different phases and I think, "Holy heck, that's a lot to process." You watch your friends going through these phases of their lives and you think, "Wow, your decision-making is really shaped by your children rather than for yourself." That's not a criticism, everyone needs to consider a lot in these types of challenges, but you just go, "Wow, if you didn't have kids it would play out so differently for you."'

She is right that you cannot be free if you are a parent. Rachel Cusk wrote in her book *A Life's Work*:

> [Birth] divides women from themselves, so that a woman's understanding of what it is to exist is profoundly changed. Another person has existed inside of her, and after the birth they live within the jurisdiction of her consciousness. When she is with them she is not herself; when she is without them she is not herself, and so it is as difficult to leave your children as it is to stay with them.

Even as your children become more independent, you are not free of them. If you are the mother, you generally move from not being able to leave the house without them because of breastfeeding, to weaning, then back to work and a slow return to 'your' life. But you are never free of your children. You still have to be there at a certain time to pick them up. You still have to come home eventually each night. You still have to get up with them in the morning. And even when they leave home, you still have to think about them.

It's difficult for those without children to grasp how every single aspect of your life is dictated by your children. It's a good reason not to have them. If you have them, you will constantly look back and be astounded at how casually you entered parenthood.

'[There's an] idea that people [who choose not to have children] actively dislike children, [but this] is actually a very small percentage. The most common reason that I can get is they don't feel maternal or paternal. It is by far the biggest factor,' says Dr Harman.

'I have started to see a rise in people saying [no for] environmental reasons, but overwhelmingly it is because they do not have a maternal feeling.'

Until coronavirus hit, there was not actually a significant number of millennials choosing not have children compared to previous generations; in fact, the birth rate had begun to lift slightly, which was in line with a trend that stretches back not just decades, but centuries. Or as Dr Harman put it, 'What might surprise a lot of people is that child freedom is not a new thing, it comes in waves.'

Usually at the start of a century, the birth rate will be low, before rising again in the middle of the century and falling again at the end. The most dominant theory for this is that, going back centuries and centuries, there is usually an economic decline at the end of the century that puts people off having children for a couple of decades.

'In the 1970s, the birth rate dropped to the lowest rate ever, and it's been dropping ever since ... Just before the pandemic hit, the birth rate had slowly begun to rise again,' Dr Harman said.

Now, she says, people are scared again and there is a confluence of reasons not to have children that has not been seen since World War Two.

'The influences go beyond the economic impacts. We are seeing decreased economic stability, increased anxiety, decreased employment and increased cross-generational social concerns (climate change plus COVID-19),' she wrote in an email after we had spoken.

'One of these factors is usually enough to see a decrease in birth rate, all four simultaneously are less common, and in the last century have only occurred twice that I can remember, that is, World War One and World War Two.

'I anticipate a VERY dramatic drop in the birth rate, which will be not just people having fewer children (which is the main reason for the drop in the birth rate for the last 20 years) but more people choosing child freedom.'

Harman attributed the brief rise in the birth rate to people changing their minds about having children and beginning to have them in their 30s. The fact most people choose to have fewer children than they did 100 years ago, however, meant the birth rate didn't rise as dramatically as it has in the past.

'The birth rate is very much a mindset thing. When we talk about the baby boom, it's not actually a baby boom, it's a marriage boom. Most babies are conceived within a formal marriage. If you look at stable de facto relationships and take those into account, as well as formal marriages, that's where most children are born,' she said.

When people feel secure, then they get married, and then comes children. When they feel insecure in the world, in the economy, then they are less likely to get married and therefore have babies.

***

In my interviews with people who had decided not to have children, they would mention lives changing, a loss of freedom, and I, at the time seven months pregnant with my second child, would think, 'At least you are realistic about it.' Or 'Yep.' I can't count the number of parents who have whispered to me with shock, 'I didn't think it would be like this.'

No matter who you are or what kind of mother you had, she is a main character in your life. Our mothers who loved us too much, our mothers who didn't love us enough, our mothers who we know like the back of our hands, our mothers who were not around when we were young, or died when we were young, or hovered over us constantly when we were young. They all leave an indelible mark. Even if intellectually you know that your own parenting set-up could be very different, scores of women I spoke to were imprinted with certain ideas of what mothering would be like, born from their experiences with their own mothers.

So many found it difficult to conceive of it a different way, even when they had different sexualities, different jobs, or different partners to their mothers.

Freya looked at her mother when she was eight and thought that child-rearing looked like a lot of 'drudgery'. Her mother had five children while her grandmother's 'biggest lament' in life was that she had not been able to have more children. An aunt of Freya's had two children who both died, while another aunt birthed twins after her husband had died. She said the family drew together to help raise the twins and 'became obsessed'. As a nine-year-old, Freya grew sick of hearing about the twins' milestones and what they had been up to.

'It was so boring to me, I remember it very clearly. And I know this sounds quite precocious, but I was desperately aware that women were meant to be mothers and I was consciously preparing myself for that eventuality, even at, like, eight, nine, and I couldn't think of anything worse. It looked like hell. It looked like so much drudgery to me. And an identity that I wasn't interested in,' she says.

She was about eight years old when she was sent to a nursing home to interview an elderly resident for school and met an old woman who had never had children because she didn't like them. 'At first it just seemed like the scariest thing I could think of. "Oh my God, what do you do if you're a woman and you don't have a baby?" But the idea was really relayed to me at that moment.'

She decided soon after meeting her that she would never have children, although she did not voice this to her mother until she was 12 years old. Her mother's response was something that she would hear many times over the next decades: 'You will change your mind.' The comments intensified in her late 20s, from her family but also from the women she worked with.

'It was such a "Yay, let's all have babies" kind of environment that if I voiced my desire to be child-free, I would have been considered a monster.

'I think so many people at my work got their identity from that. And sort of like a, not a martyrdom but a statehood from having children, you know, there's so much attention around being a mother. It's like, you go from being hot to being a mother. That's the role of women. And then if you decide not to do that, then you don't have an identity anymore except for grouch or spinster.'

When I observe she realised quite early how all-consuming babies can be, she corrected me: 'motherhood', not 'babies'.

'And on the other hand, the men in my life, my father would go for months at a time on jobs that were all over the world, and then there was my mum washing fabric nappies because that was the ideal.'

It strikes me that she has not asked her mother a lot about why she made certain decisions about motherhood. There are lots of things it did not occur to me to ask my parents until I was a parent myself. Even though I lived the commitment of bathing a baby every night, having them completely reliant on me for survival, I still cannot quite comprehend that that was what was done for me, and what it was like for my parents. I still secretly think I am the centre of my parents' lives, even though my child is not the centre of mine. Like Freya's mum, my parents also opted for fabric nappies, and when I asked my dad why he didn't use disposable nappies when we were kids, he told me they were not as readily available or as cheap. But Freya thought her mum had used them because 'that was the ideal'.

Talking to Freya made me realise how possible mothering had seemed to me because of my own mother, who I still like to hold to stupid standards when evaluating her performance. She worked full-time – she worked all the time it felt like sometimes – and my dad made a lot of lunches, cooked a lot of dinners, picked us up from school. It was entirely normal to me in the 1990s that it was Dad who would plait my hair before school and Dad who watched me play hockey. He was even the first person I told when I got my period, just because he was the parent who was home at the time.

It did not occur to me that this set-up could be perceived as radical until I was well into my 20s, and when I was deciding whether or not to have a baby it did not occur to me that their father wouldn't get up in the middle of the night, change nappies, cook dinner. Raise the children as well.

I am told all the time how lucky I am that my husband parents. And I am. But jokes are made at my expense while he is praised for doing the same things I do for my children. My good friend referred to my husband as 'a single parent' because after I went back to work full-time, my husband cut back his days at work to look after our son. He takes our son to the park on weekends, makes breakfast for him every morning, takes him to childcare and, when he is home, does bath and bed time. I pick our son up every afternoon, cook his dinner the same number of nights a week as my husband, take him to the park, and do bath and bed time all the nights my husband is at work. I taught our son how to undress himself, how to get in and out of the car, how to do all the animal noises, and I read to him every day. I do all that while working full-time after spending all day almost every single day with him for 10 months after growing him in my freakin' stomach and pushing him out into the world.

But I'm the lucky one.

It's entirely possible to parent equally. (Well, after the first year when it is usually the mother who is breastfeeding and is allowed adequate time off work to care for the baby.) But it would be dishonest to suggest I am anything other than the exception to a rule that does still exist in 2020. The rule being the child is the mother's responsibility.

Not wanting to be a mother because of what it could potentially trap you into is a very good reason not to become a parent. I am the naive one when it came to that consideration.

Often when talking to women about not wanting to have children, we wound up talking about their mothers. Molly, 30, does not feel like she wants children, but she keeps thinking she will end up having them anyway. Whenever she is at the pub, a few schooners in, she will start asking parents, 'What's it like?'

'I just can't imagine making such a big decision without having massively thought it through. And then regretting having a kid, I can imagine that and I dread that ... I would just hate to have not thought it through and then realise that it's actually not for me. I'm kind of agnostic, I believe in the idea of having a child, I'd be open to changing my mind if hormones and partner and everything kind of came together in my probably mid-30s, but my starting point is that I don't want to have them and you can convince me otherwise.'

So far she has heard two people say they regret having children, but she believes her data to be slightly skewed by the fact they were both armpit deep in the 'baby does not sleep' phase. After talking around the edges of the reasons she does not want kids for 30 minutes, Molly finally revealed what she believes to be at the core of it all – her own mother. Her mother who loved her, has always been supportive of her, and who did not want her or her brothers.

'She told me recently that she didn't want to have kids and I didn't know that, I only found that out two months ago, I think. And I was like, "Whoa, OK." I think she was talking with her sisters and I was there. I don't think she realised that she had never told me that and that that might be, like, a bit of a hard thing [for me] to hear,' she said.

'I don't know whether it was really hurtful. It was just kind of like, "Ah yeah, thought so" … But you know, I think you can sense if your mum wasn't super sold on being a mum and being in that mum role. And I don't think it's damaged me in any way, but I think it's hard to be maternal when you don't have a mum who was maternal.'

Pop culture abounds with stories of men who did not want to be fathers, and stories of people with not particularly involved fathers – the uninterested dad is pretty much a standard trope. It's more normal to have a dad who isn't that keen, but it must be very strange to have a mother like Molly's, when we're told in every television show, every magazine and every book that being a mother is the most fulfilling thing ever. If your mum didn't feel that way, or didn't hide it well enough, it can be quite jarring. Although it may have meant Molly was a few steps ahead of the rest of us when it comes to the realities of mothering.

Freya praised a friend of hers for emphasising her life outside of her child, and in particular 'making sure she never cancelled plans'. Freya complained that her sister, who has two toddlers, sometimes would not return a text for weeks.

If Freya does not want to have to cancel plans because a kid has a temperature or has vomited, or a teenager promised $20 an hour didn't show up to look after the kid; if she wants to respond to texts from people she loves promptly, then she is right, she should not become a mother.

After talking to Freya, I initially wrote, 'I don't know why her comments make me defensive,' trying to be cool and self-aware by admitting that I was defensive, but that is dishonest. I *do* know why they make me feel defensive.

It is because she is right about most things. The drudgery and the repetitiveness and the loss of identity and having to be home at 7 pm every night and the loss of spontaneity and not even being allowed to sleep when you are tired. She is right. That is what it's like.

At one point I asked her, can she see what the appeal of having children is to some people?

'No. I really, really, really can't. It's a mystery to me and, like, I've read lots of articles about it because, you know, obviously I'm 35 so it's become more of a prevalent issue ... but to be honest it still sounds like a complete fucking drudgery,' she says.

'With someone who appreciates you and loves you – of course I love my mum and my grandma – but there's also a level of entitlement. There's a lot of drudgery and also there's no reward in my eyes. I'm close to my mum but I live overseas. She's got lots of friends … I don't think her life would be significantly worse without me to be honest. If she didn't know about me, not if she lost me.

'Modern motherhood demands so fucking much of people … it feels like service to a lovely dictator.'

Not only that, but you have no idea of what your child will be like.

'It terrifies me that you could have a kid and you have no idea who's coming. Like, you have a kid and you are basically inviting a tiny screaming stranger into your life that you instantly love because of hormones. I don't want to be manipulated by my hormones.

'… But the truth is, why would I take the risk when I have the best life?'

The only time Freya ever wavered in her commitment not to have children was when she miscarried a baby after an accidental pregnancy a few years ago. She was surprised to find herself upset for a week afterwards. But not enough to get pregnant on purpose.

Freya's experience echoes that of Niall, 36, who lives in Tasmania with his partner of six years, both of them originally from Ireland. He has been resolute about being child-free for most of his life, but had to think when I asked how people have reacted. It turns out not many people seem to mind that a man in his 30s does not want children. Have I ever written a less surprising sentence?

For Niall, his mental health is a big factor in not having children. He also worries about the future of the planet, the world his children would inherit and the type of parent he would be.

'Not to be flippant about it, but it stresses me out having a cat. I worry constantly about the cat's wellbeing, I'm scatterbrained and probably a selfish person in a way and I don't earn a lot of money, I never have. It would change our lifestyle completely as well,' he says.

'If we were to try and bring a child up, the happiness we predict it would bring us would be outweighed by the physical and financial and medical cost of it. The stress that it would bring me would not be outweighed by the happiness it would bring me.'

Then one day his partner told him she was pregnant.

'What do we do now?' he asked her.

'I don't know,' she responded.

Because of Tasmania's strict laws about abortion, the couple had to make a decision quickly and spent a week discussing it. Their longheld belief that they did not want children suddenly collided with the reality of a potential life growing inside her uterus.

'If you had told me beforehand that we were going to be placed in that position, then it would have been immediately obvious that we wouldn't have a child. But it wasn't as obvious as I thought it would be. It was a harder decision than I predicted it would be,' he says.

'Being on temporary visas and on the other side of the world from our families and our support networks might have influenced that as well. The fact that if we had had a child, it wouldn't have been near its grandparents or its cousins or whatever else, possibly influenced it as well, which is really sad to think of – that if we were in a different physical space, we might not have made that decision.

'But I think it was the right one. I think it would've upended our lives completely and wouldn't have had any benefit for the world, which is a bleak way of putting it, but is what I believe.'

Like Freya, he was shocked at the emotions a pregnancy provoked. Unlike Freya, he did not think he had the 'best life'.

When I originally asked Freya why she thought she had the best life, she mentioned doing her dream job in Europe with her husband by her side and the rich friendships she had cultivated. It sounded like a nice life with plenty to be satisfied with. But a day later, she messaged me. She was worried her initial answer was shallow and did not get to the crux of it.

'Of course I set my own hours, priorities, choose my company, can travel easily and spend my money at my discretion rather than on uniforms and excursions and a people-mover. But one of the things I appreciate most about being child-free is that it excuses me from the dictates of time,' she wrote.

'I think a lot of women my age have to plan their lives around having kids, balancing it with their career, looking for the right – or even just a good-enough – man, to hit certain targets by certain ages, and hope they get there before time runs out. Being child-free means life isn't a rush for me, not day to day or year to year. I think maybe it changes my relationship with and experience of time, and I like the pace. It's like everyone is running a sprint and I am on the side having a glass of wine.'

There is nothing you can do to stop the march of time. You're still going to get older, if you're lucky. Your body is still going to disappoint you, it just might be at a much later date. You may get to pass the time in a much more pleasant way without children. If you don't have children by choice, then I don't believe you will regret it. When my friends ask me questions about having children versus not having children, the deep-down truth is I think they would be happy if they had them. But I also think they would be happy if they didn't have them. There is no correct answer.

The discussion around having children or not often puts parents and non-parents in opposing camps and is far too emotionally loaded. Even the term 'child-free' is loaded. We would never say 'woman-free' or 'Black-free'. Children should not be thought of as a burden to be 'free' from. The discussion is also sometimes turned into an ideological or moral one, but not every personal choice has to have a moral imperative. Not having children is just that: not having children. It's not saving the world, or benefitting the environment; it doesn't mean you have to devote yourself to more worthy causes.

It turns out money and the future of the planet are the simple reasons not to have kids. When you just don't feel like having children, it is far more complex than the fate of the natural world and whether you can afford it.

Reasons to have children

I believe most parents regret having their children.

It may only be for a minute. It may be for a week. It may be for a year. Or more. You are allowed to complain about your children, you are allowed to talk about how difficult it is, but mostly in a kind of *noble* way. Look at this supremely difficult and kind of selfless thing I am doing, just look at it.

You're not actually allowed to talk about regretting it.

But most parents do.

Regret it.

At certain points.

So why have them?

Well. It is hard to talk about the good parts of having children without slipping into sentimentality. When I was growing up, I had no particular interest in children. I was surrounded by them: my cousins, my cousins' kids, my own younger siblings. I had so many babies come into my family so quickly that I remember how completely unremarkable the arrival of my youngest sister, Alice, was. I was in kindergarten and my teacher said to me excitedly, 'I hear you have a baby sister!' I didn't even look up from the paper I was drawing on with red crayon and shrugged. 'I already have a little sister,' I replied.

(Alice hates stories like that. She has a complex. Not so long ago, my dad, who is seemingly allergic to memories of and nostalgia about his children, became animated talking about my first steps. He described what I was wearing, what I had been doing, and what the occasion was when I stood up and walked for the first time. We were aghast to see him so thrilled, let alone thrilled about a toddler's achievement. Alice asked, 'How old was I when I first walked?' and he returned to his normal self, looking at her thoughtfully for a full minute. 'I don't know,' he said.)

When I think about why I decided to have a baby, I know the factors that were in play, but I think my reasons were not quite considered. My husband is 14 years older than me and had wanted a baby for years. He never pushed me, however, then one day I said to him, 'What if I never want a baby?'

'Well,' he said, 'then we won't have a baby. I can just be happy with you.'

He didn't pressure me, but his preferences were taken on board. I think what it actually came down to was I grew tired of thinking about it and just wanted to make a decision. For a woman in a heterosexual relationship, it really can be that elementary.

So I went off contraception and, as is customary in my obscenely large family (25 aunts and uncles, more than 30 first cousins), I got pregnant.

Even when I was pregnant, I had no maternal longings or urges. I remained unmoved by the sight of a baby. (Indeed, one of the most annoying things about becoming a mother is that people feel compelled to send you photos of random babies and, really, I still don't care.)

My mother was a midwife for decades and, though she didn't tell me until my beloved baby was six months old, she was quite concerned I was a prime candidate for postnatal depression, such was my lack of interest in becoming a mother even when I was eight months pregnant.

But then Hamish was born. The high I had for about two weeks after was unbelievable and incomparable to any high I had had before in my misspent youth. I didn't quite know how high I was at the time. I loved holding him. I loved smelling him. I loved looking at him. I loved sending photos of him to everyone I knew. It was like living enveloped in jubilation. The only thing that it was remotely like was being on MDMA.

I remember scrolling through Instagram the day after I took him home. I think I had slept for three hours and he had not been off my boob for more than 20 minutes at a time and the stitches from my vaginal birth ached.

I looked at each post feeling sorry for everyone at their Christmas parties, having their cocktails on balconies in the Australian summer, swimming in the ocean at 7.30 pm. I genuinely pitied them, that they did not have a baby, that they specifically didn't have Hamish. It's a pretty extraordinary hormonal feat.

The high didn't last, of course, and I don't want to pretend it was all a love bubble. When he was nine weeks old, I was so sleep-deprived that I began sobbing in a food court in front of my mum while I was breastfeeding. She took me back to my hometown and taught Hamish to go to sleep at 7 pm every night. That saved me in ways I probably still don't comprehend.

When Hamish was a couple of months old, my brother, Séamus, came over unannounced in the late afternoon after finishing his shift at the hospital. He opened the front door and I was sitting in my chair, crying, holding my baby, who was also crying. He walked over and lifted Hamish out of my arms, while I covered my sobbing face.

'Is there breast milk in the fridge?' he asked.

I nodded, miserable.

'Go and have a shower for as long as you want.'

I don't know how long I stayed in the shower but by the time I came out, my brother had got my baby to go to sleep and had cooked me dinner. As we were eating, the baby started crying, but, before I could be overwhelmed with my own tears again, Séamus got up from the table and went into the room and settled him.

I will never forget it.

Matt was fully present during all of this and cooked all of my meals, did night feeds, and bathed Hamish and settled him and took him out whenever he was home. But he worked long hours in the evenings, the bitchiest time for the baby. It just wasn't physically possible for him to share equally in the parenting in those early days. I don't believe just two people can look after a baby at that age. You need more.

All of these sound like pretty good reasons *not* to have a baby. I'd argue, however, that while they're not reasons *to* have a baby, they are not reasons not to. This stuff passes. Parents are quick to tell you about the lack of sleep, loss of freedom, and complete and utter surrender of privacy, but they don't often mention the good stuff.

As I was writing the above paragraph at my desk in the corner of a bedroom, I looked through the window and saw Matt pushing Hamish in the pram in the driveway. My son, now two years old, looked up and saw me and sheer delight lit up his face. 'Hello!' he called, waving and trying to jump out of his pram. 'Hello! Hello! Mama! Mama!' He smiled and waved and waved and waved.

We had seen each other about 90 minutes before.

Imagine being greeted with so much joy every day, sometimes multiple times a day. I cannot tell you how good it feels, even though I know it is literally what I am supposed to be doing. There are so many small moments in a day, sometimes in an hour, where I can feel the love inside me bulging in my veins.

As I was writing the above paragraph, he stood next to my chair vacuuming the shirt I was wearing with our expensive Dyson. But that doesn't negate anything.

What a lot of people leave out when they are telling you about the realities of parenting are the daily joys, the enthusiasm for everyday life you are given, how eating a banana can become an event, the relief of thinking so much about someone else rather than yourself.

When I was pregnant with my second baby, some of my closest friends, who are allowed to voice such things, questioned how this baby could be as good as Hamish. How could we all love another baby this much? Another baby that isn't Hamish? Wouldn't Hamish always secretly be our favourite? It was too much for a baby to live up to. But then Cormac arrived. A completely different baby with a completely different temperament and even different eyes. We were all completely besotted. Again. Against what we thought were impossible odds.

My sons are so good for me. So much better, so much more, than I could've conceived before I had them. They are the best part of my day.

I have also lost a lot. You cannot expect to keep all of the good bits of your previous life and only add good bits.

And of course Hamish won't greet me with such glee every time he sees me for the rest of his life. Especially when it's only been 90 minutes since he last saw me.

In psychologist Bruno Bettelheim's words,

> There are few loves which are entirely free of ambivalence. ... Not only is our love for our children sometimes tinged with annoyance, discouragement, and disappointment, the same is true for the love our children feel for us.

He also blamed mothers for children having autism, so a lot of his work can be safely ignored; but in the case of ambivalence and love, he wasn't wrong.

I know I will fail my sons, and our relationship is not just about how I feel about them, but also how they will feel about me. There is no hiding from your children. As they get older, they will see all the worst parts of myself, bear witness to my faults in character and probably at times focus on them at the expense of my OK traits.

I have a friend who is absolutely devoted to her son and daughter. She works part-time and spends all of her free time developing fun and educational activities for her children and thinking about what is best for them in every way.

I am sure her kids will one day say, 'My mum didn't give me enough space.' Just as I am sure my own sons will say at some point, 'My mother didn't give me enough attention, she was always busy with other stuff.'

This is the thing about your children – they see you as you are, entirely fallible but they tend to see your faults too acutely.

Of all the things I lost when I became a mother – time, being a size eight, obliviousness to true terror, an aversion to anxiety, time – I did not lose my identity. Even when breastfeeding and when going to Woolworths by myself was an ecstatic exercise in freedom, I still felt like me. I remember being home with Hamish when he was about three days old and reading the *Guardian* news app and thinking, 'Oh, I can still read.' Of course I could still read. But the way some parents had spoken about it, I had expected my true self to be subsumed, to be drowned.

Instead, I kept across the news because I was still interested in the news. I continued to read books because I still loved books – there is actually a lot of time to read, particularly with your first baby, because there is a lot of sitting around with them attached to your chest and not much else to do.

I had vulnerable points, times when I thought maybe I had been obliterated by motherhood and was becoming boring, but what I feared more than what I thought of myself was how other people now thought of me. I was still funny, still crass, still smart, still part of the world around me. I was desperate for people to see that, worried that they would only be able to see the baby.

Along with my identity, I had also been tricked into thinking my creativity would disappear as I pushed my baby into the world.

'There is no more sombre enemy of good art than the pram in the hall,' that English literary critic, writer and prick Cyril Connelly said. Connelly sponged off his increasingly broke father and his first wife's parents to fund his 'bohemian' lifestyle, didn't have children until he was in his 50s, and still managed to produce only one novel. I don't think a pram had anything to do with that.

When author Zadie Smith was seven months pregnant, a childless male writer whose identity we can only speculate on (I have my theories) told her she must 'be worried about falling behind'. She responded: 'You must be worried about just a complete lack of human experience, that you're now going to be 40 and then 50.'

Being creative, or being thoughtful, or being whatever it is you were before you were a parent, particularly a mother, can be harder, but it's entirely possible.

The biggest adjustment I have found is that I don't get to have my 'best time of the day' to write anymore. It used to be that I wrote best first thing in the morning, but that's when Hamish wants me to make him a dinosaur toast, or read him a book, or stop him from playing with the heater, or just talk to him. Now my writing has to be done at night after he has gone to sleep, or on the train back from work, or in the hour when he's at the park, or whenever I can. Not when I want to.

You still get to be you, you're just you with a kid. But how radical to try to apply that to your own mother. Can you imagine her as a fully formed human with an interior life beyond her children? Ridiculous.

***

Twin ideas often tied to parenthood are those of completion and learning what love is. It is not uncommon to hear people say, 'I did not know what love was before I had a child.'

Of course, usually, if your circumstances growing up were not too extreme and grim, you knew what love was. But you didn't know what it was for the survival of another human being to be so dependent on you. Maybe you didn't ever experience the illusion you could shape someone (you can influence someone, sure, but shape? Within three months of your child talking, I guarantee they will express desires you completely disagree with and are foreign to you), but that's different.

Just as loving your sibling is different to loving your lover, the love you have for your child is – as far as I can tell – unique. You probably wouldn't forgive your sister as many times if she screamed at you for putting the wrong Peppa Pig shirt on her or if she threw the dinner you made at the wall because a sausage touched a potato, but that is separate to 'not knowing what love is'.

A lot of mothers feel pressure to be completed by their children. Or even go into motherhood with the expectation of being completed. But that shit's hard. You can't just have a kid and be completed. You still have to do the work on yourself, with or without parenthood. You let your kid define you and pretty soon, sooner than you think, your new identity is going to leave home or perhaps even come to resent you.

It is a big, big, big love, though. At times a suffocating love. At times the most annoying love you will encounter, ever, easily. It's one of the main reasons to have a baby, actually. It's hard, though, because they are never going to love you the same way. They can't love you the same way.

If our children loved us in the way we love them, then the world would not be able to exist. Everyone would be too paralysed with terror and devotion. They wouldn't leave home and they wouldn't be able to survive when parents died, and we have to die. (I know some parents outlive their children. I cannot fathom.)

It's hard to write about this love, because 1) it is a love mixed with so much sacrifice and 2) pretty much everybody sounds deranged when they try to describe the love they have for their children.

I thought it was a love that would become more manageable over time, but a woman told me she feels the same way about her adult children that she did when they were toddlers. It seems impossible. If this is true, how does my father ever stop hugging me? How does my mother survive months without seeing me? How do my parents just go to work, go to the shops, see their friends and have a life, knowing their children are somewhere else, possibly making bad decisions? Drinking? Probably with people who wouldn't throw themselves in front of a car to protect them? How do you exist knowing they are boiling kettles by themselves thousands of kilometres away, and anything could happen with a boiling kettle? (I will have to ask them one day when I remember to call.)

Sound deranged? It's completely deranged. That's how deranged it feels to love your kid. That's why we all sound so lame when we talk about our kids. Even when we are not thinking about them, we are always thinking about them.

It's also disconcerting to have them and not feel fundamentally changed. My life is fundamentally changed, but I still feel like the same woman as before. Still wasting time scrolling online, still having too many wines sometimes on a Saturday night with mates, still doing stupid things. I somehow thought that would evaporate when I came into the very real responsibilities of parenthood.

Just after my child turned one, my husband took him to north Queensland while I still had to work. I went on the tear. Straight back to my habits pre-pregnancy, pre-breastfeeding, pre-parenthood. Sure, I had work, but that didn't stop me partying until 3 am, drinking gallons at dinner parties, eating pizza over the sink for breakfast and sleeping in until 10 am when I could. It's amazing how quickly we can return to our base selves.

I also talked about my son. A lot. About how great having him was, how having a kid is the best, how everyone should have one. I think it's one of the only times I've ever directly said to someone that they should have a kid. Even though this particular person had not asked me.

I am usually careful not to give such advice, even when my friends are talking to me about deciding whether or not to have kids. It's hard not to sound preachy, or desperately like I am trying to indoctrinate them. Besides, they will never have *my* kid; their kid could be a dud.

Heather Havrilesky, an advice columnist who writes *The Cut*'s 'Ask Polly' column, did not have any such qualms when a reader wrote in and asked if she should have a child.

'It was difficult and also incredible,' Havrilesky wrote of early parenthood.

'It was taxing and also glorious. Having kids is hard to describe for that reason. Not that many things are as dramatically good and stressful at the same time. It's a little bit like a good marriage. You feel some hatred and some love, together. It's like being with your family of origin, or traveling with your best friends. It's incredible and you'd also like to murder someone.'

She is right.

***

Not everyone has the overwhelmingly positive experience of parenthood that I had. There are two essential factors not quite within a mother's control. The first is whether you have a true and equal co-parent, and the second is the baby you are given. I say having a true and equal co-parent is not quite within a mother's control because the way some partners, mostly men, can behave after a child is born can be totally different to what was thought and agreed upon prior. At times I have found my child overwhelming, but it was never a constant. That would've been different if his father didn't get up in the night with him. Even when I was breastfeeding, Matt would take the baby afterwards and put him to sleep so I could just go back to bed. After we started mixed feeding, he would take wake-ups before 3 am-ish and I would take anything from 5 am. If there was a wake up between 3 am and 5 am, then we would have the classic stand-off of who could pretend to be asleep the longest (me!).

If one of us was particularly exhausted, then they would get to sleep and the other would take the baby. Matt was working full-time but it was an office job. Any parent who has stayed home at any length with a child can tell you which is harder – going to the office on almost no sleep or looking after a baby for the entire day and evening. Going into the office can be like Christmas when you have a kid.

I've heard a lot of women say their partner has to work and that's why they don't get up at night. To those partners I say, if you are not operating heavy machinery or doing surgery on someone, suck it up and have five coffees. You're a parent. You'll deal.

The baby you are given is much more difficult to reckon with.

If you have a high-needs baby, then I cannot help you. Not many people can. Sometimes you have a baby who will not stop screaming, for months, and refuses to sleep. Often those babies have undiagnosed reflux, but they also can just be high maintenance. My deepest sympathies are with you and I honestly think we should honour those parents with some medals. Plural.

Most of the time, however, if you have an average baby, they scream in the first three months and then it gradually lessens. You can teach them to be OK with various people holding them. Some form of sleep training will eventually work. You can teach them to cope with sitting by themselves.

The most valuable lesson I learned was you can ignore your baby. You can put them down to eat lunch, even if they don't like it. You can let them amuse themselves for a bit. You don't have to give them constant attention. They'll be fine.

In a pretty short space of time, parenting has gone from something that pretty much everyone did to a *project.* One of the fantastic upsides of this is that children are often listened to a lot more now than even 15 years ago. They're believed.

A downside is an absurd amount of pressure is piled on parents to do everything that is best for the child, quite often at their own expense. We have a duty to the child, for sure. But it's also OK to do things because *you* want to do them. Because you enjoy them.

I know one woman who, when her baby was three months old, would listen only to The Wiggles and podcasts for babies, do projects with the baby, read only books for the baby, and start the entire routine again the next day.

Let me assure you: you absolutely do not need to do projects with a three-month-old.

Cuddle the three-month-old, feed the three-month-old, get the three-month-old to sleep however you can, talk to the three-month-old. That's pretty much all you need to do. I would read some kids' books to my baby, but mostly I would read out whatever I was reading, if I read it out loud at all.

Once her son was two years old, my friend would often say how differently she would treat the first six months if she had another child. Mainly she would listen to the music she wanted to for as long as possible.

I didn't play kids' music for my kid until he could ask for it. You have years of listening to The Wiggles ahead of you, so keep playing Kanye for those first few months.

Boredom is good for the kid, probably. That's what I've often told myself. I did not burden myself with trying to keep my baby engaged for all the minutes of the day.

The secret to happy parenting is having low expectations of yourself. You don't have to raise a genius. Your kid doesn't need to know the alphabet at two years old. Feed them and listen to them and, most importantly, love them (actually, maybe feeding is most important). They will be fine.

When parents regret having their children, which every parent does, they are mourning not just their former life, but their youth. They are mourning something they could never go back to, even if they never had children. It is just one of many things they mourn that they wouldn't have had, even without children – except for money, they would absolutely have way more money if they didn't have children.

It's the same as when people don't know if they are unhappy because of their long-term relationship or if it is just easier to blame their partner instead of looking too closely at themselves.

As Taffy Brodesser-Akner wrote in *Fleishman is in Trouble*:

What were you going to do? Were you not going to get married when your husband was the person who understood you and loved you and rooted for you forever, no matter what? Were you not going to have your children, whom you love and who made all the collateral damage (your time, your body, your lightness, your darkness) worth it? Time was going to march on anyway. You were not ever going to be young again. You were only at risk for not remembering that this was as good as it would get in every single moment – that you are right now as young as you will ever be again. And now. And now. And now and now and now.

It has always been worth it. What was the alternative for me? A quiet house? An ordered life?

So have the baby. Love the baby. Fight with the baby (juvenile, but you will do it). Read to the baby sometimes. Ignore the baby sometimes. Cuddle the baby. Choose the baby's outfits while you can. Enjoy the baby. Regret the baby, sometimes. But have the baby.

My money and my routines

I have a healthy obsession with other people's routines. What they eat, how they spend their money, what their day looks like – I love to know all of it, whether they're an anonymous office worker in Sydney or a CEO who made $100 million before they turned 35. I will greedily read money diaries, 'my day on a plate'–type food diaries, and 'How I get it done'–type recounts on what their average day looks like to glean how they live. Or, at least, how they pretend they live for the purposes of published interviews.

I say 'healthy obsession' because I have never read a single word about someone else's habits that have made me change my own. I've taken advice, sure, but that's not what these accounts are. They're a sanitised window into how other people function. I read them because one day I might stumble across one that contains *the secret*. The thing that will tell me how to be self-disciplined. The thing that will make me into a successful person.

I read them to feel better about myself – at least I am not so deprived that I think two squares of dark chocolate is a 'treat'. I read them to kid myself – wow, this woman spends $62 a week on takeaway coffees, how extravagant. I'm just going to pretend that I don't sometimes spend $16 on noodles at lunch.

I also read them because if you're not careful, then giving an insight into your habits can reveal so much: your insecurities, how your mother spoke to you when you were a teenager, the supposed gaps in your education, whether or not you are a serious person, your deepest desires.

A WEEK OF SPENDING IN MY NORMAL LIFE

I get paid fortnightly and put $1200, which is roughly half of my pay, into a joint savings account I share with my husband. Out of this account comes our rent, mortgage repayments after rental income on our apartment, childcare and other bills – the boring but essential stuff – which add up to about $4500 a month. We usually put more into it than what comes out, so we are saving about $700 a month between us.

Here's where the rest of it goes:

Monday
I take the train to work (**$3.61**). On my way to the office, I duck into the supermarket to buy:
A loaf of bread: $3.90
A packet of plastic cheese: $4.20

Two packs of Lurpak butter on special: $10

This, along with the Vegemite I already have on my desk, will be enough for breakfast every day for a couple of weeks. I love leftover Thai for breakfast, and I have tried cooking extra vegetables the night before and heating those up in the morning for a much more virtuous breakfast, but I have eaten Vegemite and cheese on toast for breakfast roughly 300 days of the year for the past 18 years. It's easy, it's cheap, it's delicious every time.

I try to make it at my desk so I don't have to make small talk in the kitchen about what I'm eating. If I put the plastic cheese on my toast there, then at least three different people will say, 'Oh my God, you're *eating* that cheese!' Talking about food in the work kitchen should be banned. Five days a week for 40 years, we utter the words, 'Yum, that smells good,' 'Leftovers?', 'That makes mine look boring,' and 'Oooooh, what have you got there?' But if we banned talking about food, I suppose we would be trapped talking about the weather, the commute and other people's boring children five days a week for 40 years.

I also drink plunger coffee at my desk each morning, so every couple of months I buy a bag of ground coffee for $25. Not today, though.

I eat leftovers for lunch and take the train home at the end of the day (**$3.61**).

When I get home, Matt makes us all dinner. I don't cook. It's not that I can't cook. Of course I can cook, almost everyone who has been self-sufficient since they moved out of home as a teenager can cook. But I don't like it and Matt does, so I don't cook. I love food, but cooking is a hassle and, contrary to the current propaganda around it, extremely boring.

Total spend for the day: $25.32

Tuesday

Return fare to and from work: $7.22

A grilled chicken banh mi for lunch: $12, at the café I have been going to for seven years (!) where all the staff greet me by name: Anna. When I first went to the café, I did not know that I would be eating there for years or that the staff were so enthusiastic about learning their beloved customers' names. So when they took my name for the order, I said what I always say: Anna. If I say my name, it usually goes like this:
'Bridie.'

'What?'

'Bridie.'

'What?'

'Bridie! B-R-I-D-I-E.'

And then my coffee goes cold as I stand next to the counter while they call out for Brodie.

Anna is my sister's name so I always respond when I hear it called out and everyone can say and spell it first go. So seven years ago, I ordered a salad sandwich and said my name was Anna, and now every week when I walk into the café, at least one staff member, but usually two, says, 'Hi Anna! How are you going?'

It's too late to do anything about it.

After lunch, I take a detour by my favoured manicure place for **a $21 gel polish**, which I get every two or three weeks.

Dinner is cooked for me again.

Total spend for the day: $40.22

Wednesday
Train fare to work: $3.61

Babysitter day! **$90 for three hours** of freedom after work. When people casually tell me to 'just get a babysitter', I want to kick them in the shins. Some of them complain about being invited to their friends' houses for dinner all the time instead of going out. They don't realise that if their friend has small children, they are already paying $90-ish to hang out with them when they 'just get a babysitter'.

I get a babysitter every Wednesday because I usually don't finish work on time to be able to pick up my toddler. And as long as she's picking him up, I might as well get her to watch him for a few hours to make it worth her while. Also, I love going to the pub on a Wednesday.

A 20-pack of Winfield Gold: $31. I don't smoke. Except for tonight. I'll just have a few tonight. Then I will throw out this pack. And never smoke again. I can't believe it's $31 for a pack of 20! I remember when I could get those cheap Coles packs for $12. I wonder if they still sell them. I should check next time I'm at the supermarket. No I shouldn't. Because I don't smoke. That's why I'm always spending $31 on a 20-pack, because I buy them on a whim when walking past a 7-Eleven on the way to the pub. Because I don't smoke.

Beer: oh, I don't know, maybe $2132? Not really, but it feels like it the next day. It's actually about $72 on beers and burgers and chips and shouts that I'm not sure get shouted back.

I text the babysitter and tell her I will be late. She's cool with it, but it's another **$30** out of my budget. I still catch a train home to save **$21** on an Uber, but, for those few beers after work, the total ends up being **$230.22.** This is the burden of mothers. Mothers who don't smoke.

Thursday
Return fare to and from work: $7.22

Bad decisions, bad decisions, bad decisions. A week that began in almost a monastic way has been blown out by the need for bacon for breakfast (**$9**) and spicy dumplings, noodles and a Diet Coke for lunch (**$21**).

While the flesh is so weak, my mate texts me the link to an online Ganni sale and I buy **a blazer for $160**. That used to be so much money to me, but now I can spend it on a whim, hungover. The blazer is reduced from $600, though, so I've actually saved $440.

Matt is at work and has left me dinner to heat up in the fridge. But I don't feel like chicken green curry, so I walk Hamish to the chicken shop and we get chips and burgers for dinner (**$15**). (It's a proper suburban chicken shop where the prices don't make your eyes water.)
Total spend for the day: $212.22 (but remember, $440 saved).

Friday
Back on the train to work (**$3.61**). Back to Vegemite on toast for breakfast. Matt made me a sandwich last night and left it in the fridge for me to take to work. Yes, I even don't make my own sandwiches. Die mad about it, I don't care.

At 2 pm, I inspect the charity chocolate box and pay **$4 for a $1.50 packet of M&Ms** because it's for charity, because I can't be bothered to walk downstairs to the convenience store, and also to make up for the other times I raid the charity box and am short of change.

Back home on the train (**$3.61**), I pick up my son and take him on our weekly trip to Dan Murphy's. These outings may become a story about his insane mother for him to regale others with when he's older. As Marguerite Duras noted: 'I believe always, or almost always, in all childhoods and in all the lives that follow them, the mother represents madness. Our mothers always remain the strangest, craziest people we've ever met.' Or maybe taking him to the liquor store every week as a toddler is benign compared to the other stuff he will remember. It's massively unfair that I don't get to dictate what he takes from his childhood and what he leaves behind. **Semi-decent bottle of prosecco: $18**

One of the traditions from my childhood that I have carried into my own child-rearing is no cooking on Friday night! No cooking any night for me, but no cooking for anyone on Fridays. I pay for the **large supreme pizza** for me and Matt and the **medium margherita** for the toddler: **$41**. It occurs to me for the first time that this might be expensive. I think I stopped knowing what was cheap pizza and what was expensive pizza about the same time we moved into a house so nice it had air conditioning. **Total spend for the day: $70.22**

Saturday

Leftover pizza for breakfast and plunger coffee at home. We take the toddler to the park and I buy a couple of newspapers on the way (**$8.20**), even though I will still read most of the news on my phone. On the way home I pay **$2.50 for a babyccino**, which is CRIMINAL for a bit of frothed milk, and **$9 for two banh mis**, which is how much they should always cost.

It is my friend's birthday and she's having a party at her house, which means eating dinner beforehand and BYO booze. I have forgotten to get her a birthday present so, after we get home, I drive 25 minutes to a pretty fancy florist and spend **$60 on flowers**. She's worth it and I figure I won't be spending much on going out. On the way home, I pick up **two bottles of nice champagne for $120**. She's worth it and I figure I won't be spending much on going out.

We have a nice family dinner together and I get ready to go out while the toddler gets put to bed. Carrying the flowers and champagne, I decide against catching the train and get an Uber instead (**$23**). I figure I won't be spending much on going out.

Total spend for the day: $222.70, $203 of which I justified by 'not spending much on going out', thereby spending more than I would have going out.

Sunday

I crawl out of bed in the morning and miserably eat some French toast and coffee while watching *Peppa Pig*. Matt is working today so I lounge around letting The Wiggles parent my child before he goes for a sleep. When he wakes up, I take him to his best friend's house so he's entertained. We order lunch on UberEats – my friends wave away my offer to contribute – and we sit around sharing hot chips with the boys and gossiping. When we get home, I make peas and sausages for dinner and climb into the bath with Hamish, where we listen to Taylor Swift's album *Lover*. After the toddler is asleep, I browse online for a bit and leave a cart of books unbought on Booktopia.

Total spend for the day: $0

***

As you can see my best intentions quickly unravel as the week goes on. It inevitably ends with me saying, 'I'll do better next week.' I'll buy fewer lunches, I won't shop online, I'll spend less on booze – my weekly resolutions are usually variations on these themes. I have no credit card debt and have paid cash for everything from our car to three out of the last four holidays, so my spending isn't outrageous. But, as with exercise, eating, screen time and parenting, there is nobody I know who is completely happy with their spending habits.

I once worked with a woman who saved half of everything she was paid. When she was a kid, her parents used to give her four dollars a week in pocket money but made her save two dollars of it. She would then spend her savings at the Gold Coast Show. She said because of her parents' insistence to save, when she started working as a teenager, she saved half of every pay packet. In her 20s, she quit her job and travelled the world for years with the tens of thousands she had in the bank.

Most of what I know about money is self-taught. My parents had too many kids and too many night shifts to impart any lessons about finances. When the corrupt NSW Labor politician Eddie Obeid was sent to jail for his family's secret business dealings in Circular Quay, I marvelled on the phone to Dad that the family had reportedly earned $30 million from a single coal deal.

'Some Lebanese just know how to make money,' Dad said. 'We are not that kind of Lebanese.'

So on one hand I had to figure out my own saving and spending habits, but on the other hand I was not raised to embezzle money from the state government.

In my early 20s, I figured out the best way for me to save money was to put my savings into an account that wasn't easily accessible on the day I got paid. The most credit card debt I ever had was about $1200, because I knew I couldn't trust myself with higher limits.

My brother, Séamus, has strict fortnightly budgets he follows, written out in his absurdly tiny handwriting in Fabriano notebooks my sister buys for him. He even budgets in blowouts. My younger sister, Anna, has gone from corporate jobs, to bartending, to the dole and back to corporate life and pub work throughout her 20s. She can easily live on whatever she's getting paid at the time, whether it's minimum wage or six figures. As far as I can tell, my youngest sister, Alice, spends her entire paycheck within two days of getting paid, every time. My friend Rick grew up very poor and has borrowed money from me so many times I have lost count, despite earning significantly more than me for years. When he's in money, he wants to empty the accounts so fast he once almost bought me a $400 lawnmower just because he walked past it. My other friend Kylie also grew up quite poor and bought an apartment in Sydney with her partner when she was only in her 20s, thanks to how careful she is with money.

Revealing how you spend your money is more intimate than revealing anything about your sex life. It's about how you spend your days, how you eat, how comfortable or uncomfortable you are with yourself, how you live.

***

The other eternally popular look at how people spend their days are diaries about, well, how people literally spend their days. Money diaries tend to be written and read by young women, but daily diaries have a broader appeal and usually a less vicious response. Anyone can write a money diary, but rundowns of people's work day or daily habits are usually confined to successful and/or rich people. It's how we know so many CEOs are stupidly early risers. But those habits are not for normal people. If we got up at 4.30 am for an hour of tennis, we would be asleep at our normal jobs by 10.30 am. Or we'd just be giving ourselves 2.5 hours of hitting the snooze button rather than 25 minutes.

A DAY IN THE LIFE

On mornings

Mornings used to be my best time of the day. I would get up between 5.30 am and 6 am and not look at my phone. Then I would get outside for a run. Or make a coffee and jump right into writing for an hour before my husband got up.

Now, however, the mornings are more hectic. I shower before I go to bed and sleep as late as I can – about 7 am – then I'm up and out the door to work in 30 minutes. My husband does our toddler in the mornings and I do most evenings because he's at work.

I listen to ABC Radio National all morning, and on the train I read the news, trying to get some ideas up to commission before the morning conference at work. I try to also use the train journey to start on my emails, but usually end up flicking through a couple of social media apps and checking into my group chat. My group chat has about 16 people in it, though a few drop in and out depending on work. It goes all day, every day. We talk shit, share memes, post links to news, gossip, occasionally have existential discussions, then get back to memes. I've been in it for five years now and there are people posting in it every single day. It is easily my biggest time-suck.

On how I write my books

People always want to know, how do you write a book? Well, the simple answer is you sit down, almost every day, and write a book. The harder answer is you become OK with nothing turning out the way it was supposed to and never being happy with what you have done.

I write my books hour by hour. My limit is about 2000 words a day before I am basically just mashing the keyboard, something I have learned through trial and error. I look to the week ahead and pick the days I'll be able to sit at my desk and write, usually for an hour at a time, then I sit at my desk and write for those hours. Sometimes I have more than an hour and will set a word-count goal but mostly, between full-time work, parenting, friends and having a life, I just have an hour. If I sit down at my desk for enough of those hours, eventually a book begins to take shape. I don't enjoy that hour exactly, but I love the feeling afterwards. It's worth it for the feeling afterwards.

When I was finishing my first book, Séamus lived with us for a couple of months. He is an ICU nurse in one of the biggest trauma units in our state. He would walk in the door in the morning, at the end of a 12-hour night shift, and I would shut the hell up about any thoughts I had that what I was doing was difficult. It's hard at times to write a book. It's not that hard, though.

On managing emails

I have a simple system for managing my emails that absolutely does not work, but I have not come up with a better one. Really, I don't manage my emails at all. Even my boss has to sometimes chase up a reply from me, I am that terrible at emails.

I am instantly suspicious of anyone who says they are on top of their emails. There isn't really anyone in the world who could possibly be on top of their emails. They are either lying or they are spending way too much time on their emails instead of doing real work, or thinking, or bonding with their loved ones, or making delicious snacks. There is too much you have to give up to get on top of your emails.

I have notifications on for my email and I will either respond to someone in 90 seconds, or in 32 days, or never. Those are the three options. When I see an important email, I either respond immediately, or, if I am not doing something more important, like real work or making a delicious snack, I star it. My intention is then to go through my starred emails at 3 pm that day or first thing the next morning. That sounds like a system that could probably work.

Instead, I get distracted and only remember to go through my starred emails six days later, and then feel a deep sense of shame I have not responded to the emails more promptly, and then exit my starred folder because of how bad I feel, and the starred emails keep piling up.

So if you're waiting for me to respond and I haven't done it within 90 seconds, then there is still a chance for you in 32 days. Otherwise try emailing me again, give up, or hope you run into me in the tea aisle of the supermarket and we can discuss your issue/complaint/hopes/dreams then.

On sleep

I am a champion sleeper. I am such a champion sleeper that, after my first child turned one and there was much less danger of him dying in his sleep and he didn't need to be fed in the middle of the night to survive, I could sleep through him crying. I've lost count of the number of times I've said, 'Wow, it's great he slept through the night!' only to be informed by his father he actually yelled for 90 minutes and I didn't even stir.

Since I was a child, I have laid down in bed, closed my eyes, fallen asleep and woken eight to nine hours later. Sleeping is my superpower. I didn't know it was a superpower until I was well into my 20s and began to realise all of the props and rituals many of my fellow millennials were using to sleep. One of my closest friends needs ear plugs and a face mask, and will still wake every two hours. I have friends who listen to podcasts every night, friends who play sitcoms in the background and friends who need to put their phone in another room for at least an hour before they lie down.

My world-class ability to sleep means I handled the first few months of a baby very, *very* badly. I took being woken at 2 am much too personally.

But other than that, I love sleep and it loves me. I manage to get enough sleep by going to bed about

10 pm most nights and simply sleeping through my kid waking up. I highly recommend it.

On partying

One of the most depressing and lamest things about entering your early 30s is that you have to prioritise. You have a job, you have bills, you have rent or a mortgage, you have family commitments, you're expected to bring salads to Sunday afternoon barbecues. You have to figure out what's important to you and make sure you make time for it or you'll lose the dregs of your youth to piling obligations.

Making time for what makes you happy means making time for reading, for romance, for long meandering walks, for your hobbies that will have no public recognition or discernible outcome. For me, that means making time for partying. It's something I have balanced since I was a model student topping multiple subjects in my high school while getting absolutely wrecked most weekends at the local pub. You have to be careful not to become a bit of a joke as you get older, but mostly people marvel at how I have the time to get loose.

About once a month, I go out and I go out properly. How do I work full time, parent, be a good friend, tend to my relationship *and* party? You have to make the time for what you love, and I love sinking schooners with my friends; I love standing in my mate's courtyard at 2 am talking complete bullshit with someone I have met that night; I love dancing in the middle of hundreds of other sweaty bodies.

I also do not demand perfection from myself in any of my roles. That's a very easy way to be miserable.

You don't have to achieve anything

I don't know when it started but, when I'm lying in bed at night, I like to tick off what I achieved that day. I have an ever-evolving to-do list in the Notes app of my iPhone, and I literally tick off the tasks once they are completed. Usually, I try to get at least three things off the list in a day, which includes things such as '30 minutes of barre' and 'call this person you really don't want to call for work', drab domestic stuff like 'change the sheets' and fun domestic stuff like 'look up resorts in Port Douglas'.

I feel compelled to justify the hours. It's not enough to go to work and earn some money, to pay the rent and read my kid some books and get through the day. I have to *feel* productive.

It seeps into everything; even on holidays, I like to spend the first two days walking 20 kilometres across cities, looking at a painting or two so I can say to someone, anyone, 'Look, I didn't waste it, I did this and I did that.' Then I can relax. Even my relaxation has to be factored into some sort of productivity, it has to be earned. I explore the city the right way and then I relax the right way, sitting next to a pool, reading a clever or zeitgeisty or cleverly zeitgeisty bit of literature, drinking delicious cocktails.

It's easy to blame something obtuse like 'the culture' or 'capitalism' for this constant tabulation. Waving your hands in the general direction of something big and saying, 'Oh, I am like this because of neoliberalism' makes you sound faintly intellectual. Like you know the reason you are the way you are.

I don't really know why am I the way I am, though. Is it because I am a classic eldest child? Is it because I really want to make my mum proud? Is it because I like to be admired? Is it just vanity? Or is it scarier and more overwhelming than that? Do I need my life to *mean* something?

For most of us, the answer to all of the above is yes. It can be easy to blame the culture, because that is also correct. We feel the need to prove our worth. I've seen it everywhere for years. Blatantly in posts about early morning exercise, and hobbies that involve making tables, even in 'reading stacks' posted on Instagram. Reading books, which used to be filed neatly under 'for enjoyment', has morphed into something to prove you are keeping up. Neatly stacked books litter my social feeds, and no matter whether they are marked 'to read' or 'have read', the formula is always the same. New releases, classics, old cult favourites, a mix of women and POC authors, everything just so. We can't just read what we want for pleasure now; even our books have to be 'correct'. My New Year's resolution last year was to not read any new releases. I had found myself in a spiral of the latest non-fiction and novels, so I could say I had read them, so I could be part of the discussion when someone raised the latest buzz book.

A colleague wanted to know how I managed to 'fit' reading books into my life, but it is one of the few things where no effort is required on my behalf. No habit had to be formed; I just like reading. It's easy to ignore the partner, ignore the dishes and ignore sleep when you truly love doing something. It just gets done.

But I had warped this into something I was getting done the right way, with the right books.

Cooking is a daily necessity for most people, and another once-enjoyable thing that has turned into a Doing It Right value-add. It used to be you made dinner, and that was it. Now there's Ottolenghi recipes to tick off and dinners photographed on clay plates in muted colours. There's recommended recipes and viral recipes and it's relentless, it's just so relentless. I know people who get the same easy enjoyment from cooking that I get from reading, but now we find we have to do it a certain way. Those of us for whom cooking is utilitarian now get to feel bad they don't enjoy their chore. There are few simple pleasures left that we don't feel some kind of need to excel at.

***

In February 2020, I ended up in hospital with chest pains while I was pregnant. I was ordered on to bed rest and a further check-up with my doctor. When I walked into the GP's office, she asked me how I was and I started sobbing. The kind of heaving, full-body sobbing that completely takes over. I couldn't speak, I could barely breathe.

The clock ticked past the time allotted for the appointment and I still had not stopped crying. I tried to explain why I was crying, but I could not. I did not exactly know why I was crying. 'Is this what it feels like to be depressed?' I asked her. I could barely get out of bed, I could barely make it to the end of the day, I was just holding on. 'I'm so overwhelmed, I'm so overwhelmed,' I said over and over and over.

After asking some questions about my mental health history (non-eventful), my toddler (not sleeping), my work (too eventful), and my previous post-partum experience (mostly dreamy), the doctor told me I was not depressed. I was just exhausted.

Just exhausted.

So exhausted she wanted to sign me off work for a fortnight.

Like heartbreak, proper exhaustion is hard to articulate if you have not experienced it yourself. It's also slightly embarrassing. I kept joking to people I had the celebrity's excuse for not working.

On bed rest, I made sure I didn't just lie in bed staring at the ceiling, as if I could *waste* bed rest. I read six books in ten days. I slept too, because my doctor had told me to, so it could be secretly filed into my list of achievements for the day, my doctor-ordered sleep. I also set goals of how many words to write a day. I couldn't just lie on the couch and watch *Downton Abbey*.

I got better that February, just in time for the world to change, again.

As I emerged from the depths of an exhaustion that put me in hospital, a pandemic swept across the globe. I did not know if my husband and I would have jobs at the end of it. I did not know if my father would work again, I did not know what would happen to my brother, working as a nurse in an ICU, or to my mother, working as a nurse in my hometown. Yet I still felt compelled to tick things off a list. To achieve things each day.

During lockdown, work was very intense but I also ticked off Zoom Pilates classes and a certain amount of phone calls a week with my family and friends. God forbid a little global health pandemic and pregnancy let some things fall by the wayside for a bit.

I was not the only person feeling the demand to be productive during the pandemic. For a little while, it became an opportunity people were supposed to seize. The *New York Times* was filled with articles on how to best light yourself for video meetings and what your routine at home should look like.

People were baking their own sourdough, posting photos of their stacks of books, and signing up to Zoom yoga classes at home, and suddenly everyone knew that Shakespeare wrote *King Lear* while in quarantine during the plague.

We were not permitted to just survive; as always, we had to thrive.

At the same time, at the beginning at least, our attention spans were shattered.

We knew we were expected to use the time *well*, but many of us just wrote texts to each other about how we couldn't focus on anything. We were all glued to our phones, watching the world come apart in real time. We developed a collective hypervigilance. Instead of standing at the front fence and keeping watch for the enemy to crest the horizon, we were making sure we knew what COVID-19 was doing at all times. Now Tom Hanks has it. Now 10,000 people are dead in New York. Now they don't have enough ventilators for the people who need them from Italy to England. We could not look away from the news.

The hypervigilance was exhausting and disorientating. Now it's easy to see why we were like that, but when you're living through it there is no time for a cool assessment of the situation. A cool assessment of how and why you are freaking the fuck out.

In the *Guardian*, Rebecca Solnit compared it to pregnancy:

> [When you're pregnant, your] body is growing, healing, making, transforming and labouring below the threshold of consciousness. [During the pandemic,] our psyches were doing something equivalent. We were adjusting to the profound social and economic changes, studying the lessons disasters teach, equipping ourselves for an unanticipated world.

We didn't know this, though; what we knew was that we were not doing the global health pandemic *correctly*.

I still felt it was important to strive, to achieve, to write my silly little words on my silly little keyboard while outside my window the world changed. Just like there is a correct way to dress, a correct hairstyle to have and correct opinions to have (pithy, never sentimental), there was a correct way to be when life had fundamentally shifted.

We had been expected to spend our time correctly before the coronavirus, it was not a phenomenon that arose out of the pandemic, but it became stark during it when we were all at home, thinking about what to do with the time, and concluding we should be improving.

People seemed to forget it was a global crisis. The world was tough enough before the crisis; it was hard enough to thrive before, let alone during one.

In April 2020, journalist Anne Helen Petersen was quoted in the *New York Times* saying, 'either you give up or you feel bad about it all the time'. I think a lot of people did both. Even as the headlines of self-help stories changed from 'How to be productive' to 'You don't need to be productive', we gave up, but we felt bad about it too.

We'd become used to busyness being a boast, a sign of our self-worth. You could see it in everything from social media posts about how we were spending Saturday mornings to mothering. No longer just content to watch our kids grow, to provide them food, shelter and love, there's a booming online community for those who want to make everything a lesson. To show they are engaged with their children almost every hour of the day. They have thought of everything from making sure books face out so kids can see the covers, to creating mini-kitchens so their two-year-old can fetch their own lunch snack.

If we do not have children to make ourselves busier than we need to be, then we have work or social schedules or hobbies that are not just for quiet enjoyment but culminate in an amateur art show, a stage performance, a tangible thing we will use like a vase or a knitted beanie.

Instead of hobbies, now we have 'side hustles' and a new burden: to be competent enough at the things you do for pure joy so that they too become work. If you enjoy something, but you suck at it, then you are not just risking 'being bad at something', you are risking humiliation. There is democracy in this risk, though. You can be Jim Carrey trying out painting to get over a bad relationship and be derided by an art critic as making art that 'would be turned down if he offered it to a Salvation Army store'.

Or you can be an amateur baker who posts their creation on Facebook and ends up on a Twitter account with more than 200,000 followers for, as they describe it, 'cakes with threatening auras'.

Why are we like this? We like to pretend we have control. Control over our lives, our impulses, where we live, our happiness. As if there are not a thousand other factors, in play from the day we are born, which can dictate our dumb luck.

COVID-19 shattered that illusion of control. It was a shitty time.

We were learning what did and didn't matter, and it was a lot more comforting when we thought things mattered that didn't. That was a luxury. A lovely one.

Instead, we had to learn everything can be taken from you. I missed my trivial grievances.

The things that I missed being annoyed by included but were not limited to:

- A cancelled train
- Crowded pubs where I couldn't find a table
- Thinking the next morning about how I should have left the party at midnight, not 3 am
- Tedious playgrounds
- Fun invites when I already had another thing booked
- Not being invited to fun things my friends were invited to
- My friend being sloppily drunk
- My mum
- Friends being late.

The things I missed being worried about included:

- Can we afford to move to a nicer house?
- Do I like my job?
- Am I too addicted to Instagram? (Instagram became so boring when everyone was in quarantine that it was almost obsolete for me.)

I missed not thinking about the health of my brother, who nursed in ICU, and my parents and my aunts and my uncles and everyone who I loved, who were not old but were over 60.

I was relieved that not all of my fears and concerns became so *worthy*, however. After the first initial weeks,

I returned to being preoccupied with gossip, judging my friends for drinking too much and rolling my eyes at people's sourdough starters. I just also had some real problems too.

Of course, I feel I should add a caveat here. What about poor people! What about POC! What about single people! What about infertile people! What about mothers with postnatal depression! What about people who live in a yurt for 17 days of the year! What about people who have less than a 23-month age difference with their brother!

I don't think the concerns of someone else are more noble than mine. I don't subscribe to the view there are correct and incorrect things to be preoccupied with. There are so many people who have it much harder than I do; a lot of aspects of my life are trivial. There are so many people who have it easier than I do; a lot of aspects of all our lives are trivial.

We are all allowed to fret about sex, how we look, if our best friend is better friends with someone else. It is not incorrect.

The opinions online throughout the pandemic followed a familiar cycle: first there was the take, and then there was the backlash to the take. First people suggested ways to be productive and then people started arguing there was no need to be productive.

Easy to suggest. Harder to implement. Easy to say, 'You don't need to be productive', harder to overcome a lifetime of conditioning, that niggling feeling that you should be doing more. Because it's not just about trying to maintain the illusion of control, it's also about eking out meaning from our lives.

We want our lives to mean something, and lots of us don't have religion or lifelong communities to feel tethered to anymore. We have moved more to being defined by what we have achieved, even if what we have achieved is three ten-kilometre runs in a week.

We've been conditioned to define ourselves by work, by our 'work ethics'; to think everything we have in life is something that we've earned, and the opposite, to think everything is our fault if we do not have certain things. Our fault for not working hard enough, for not being smart enough with our money. We've also been tricked into thinking we desire more than we actually need – linen bed sheets, jeans cut a certain way, fine gold necklaces with our initials on it, a jacket different from last year's jacket. When really our desires are finite, we don't need a lot of stuff, and what would make us happier is more time. There is no virtue in working hard at most jobs; it's an illusion.

Whenever I hear someone say they would keep working if they won the lottery, it makes me profoundly depressed. Working is not actually how you want to spend your time. You could be with the people you love, swimming in the ocean, having a leisurely lunch, rewatching movies from the 1990s, on a long walk – a million things that are better than working. Working 40 hours a week with two days off is a bullshit system that humans just made up. We could change it. Society could be restructured. Working sucks, it's OK to acknowledge that; acknowledging it doesn't make you a morally bereft person.

I come from a family of nurses. Both of my parents have worked as nurses, my sister has nursed in aged care since she was 16 and my brother is an ICU nurse. My nana was a nurse and three of my aunts as well. I thank them for being nurses so I can bask in the reflected glory of being able to say I come from a family of nurses.

The work they do is important and it helps people. There are not that many jobs that are genuinely important, especially in white-collar industries, although a lot of us kid ourselves that our work matters. All of my family have at different times derived different levels of satisfaction from their jobs, and there are times they enjoy it as well. They have made real differences. But I doubt they would work as many hours as they do and for as many years as they have if they didn't need the money.

This isn't to say that all work is unfulfilling and useless, but we should all be doing less of it.

From the 1830s to the 1930s, the reduction of work was one of the primary goals of society. Then all of a sudden, in the 1940s, after 100 years (ONE HUNDRED YEARS) of reducing work, it suddenly changed course. The belief that capitalism was meant to create more jobs for the economy and work could be the most satisfying part of life took hold. Historians have marked it as the end of 'the era of progressively reduced work time'.

In the 1930s, as part of the response to the Great Depression, job sharing took place across a range of industries, and W K Kellogg reduced the hours in his cereal plant to six-hour shifts. This meant that, because the plant operated 24/7, there were four shifts in a 24-hour period instead of three, meaning more people worked at the plant but they did fewer hours overall. It was a policy with resounding increases in worker productivity and happiness, but the company then spent the next few decades reversing it.

The change to four six-hour shifts wasn't done simply out of the goodness of W K Kellogg's heart; he did think there would be benefits for his company, but he was also what is a vanishingly rare breed in 2020 – a welfare capitalist. He believed that capitalism could increase happiness by leading to more freedom *from* work. That technology advances could mean less time for humans working and more free time for them. That, although their jobs could be boring – a point he personally conceded – if the hours were reduced enough, then it wouldn't matter because they would be spending more time on the things they enjoy. He even built recreation parks specifically for his employees to use in their time off. Not in some twisted attempt to get them to spend more time at work, like today's trendy tech companies stocking staff rooms with free beer and chocolate and pool tables, but because he believed in the enjoyment of free time. W K Kellogg believed he owed society something more than cereal.

The company accepted that they should also attempt to find relief for people from the Great Depression. Shorter working hours was seen as a way out, because shorter shifts meant there were more shifts to fill, thereby putting more people into jobs. The hourly rates of pay were also raised to partly compensate workers for the loss in income of going from eight-hour to six-hour days. They were also compensated with more of their time to call their own.

The movement had so much momentum that, in 1932, both presidential candidates had shorter working hours as part of their platform.

It all began to unravel when the American Federation of Labor argued policies that reduced working hours were cutting the pay of workers too much, forcing workers to shoulder all the burden of the recovery from the Depression. It then tried to put the 30-hour work week into legislation. It wasn't long before businesses were fighting the legislation of a 30-hour work week, taking up the position that the way out of the Great Depression was more work for more people, and economic expansion. President Franklin Roosevelt soon followed suit and began coming up with economic alternatives to reduced working hours. Soon 'the right to work full time' took precedence over freedom from work.

By 1935, the shorter work week had mostly been abandoned by politicians and businesses, but Kellogg's still had six-hour shifts. It had taken stock of the effects of shorter shifts on the business and found that overhead costs had been reduced by 25 per cent, labour unit costs reduced by 10 per cent, accidents reduced by 41 per cent, severity of accidents (days lost per accident) improved by 51 per cent, and 39 per cent more people were working at Kellogg's than in 1929. So more people had jobs while costs were reduced for the company and safety had improved. The company even found that, with all the savings, it could afford to pay as much for six hours of work as it had previously paid for eight.

W K Kellogg himself remained a huge advocate of reduced hours, seeing it as workers having more time to spend at church, with family, on hobbies – basically: enjoying life.

Then in 1937 the workers unionised, which surprised Kellogg. He ended up taking a step back from the company, appointing other people as directors and president, who were not so steadfast on the six-hour work day.

One of the conditions of the introduction of the six-hour work day was no penalty rates for working nights, and a bonus payment based on productivity had been introduced to replace overtime and night rates. When the union came, they began fighting for overtime and night rates on top of the bonus pay.

The bonus pay based on productivity had been introduced by W K Kellogg with the theory that workers would be happy to work harder for more money instead of longer. The union was essentially arguing for maximum pay for workers and, in the process, began bargaining away the six-hour day. So in exchange for their freedom, workers had more money to buy things they probably did not need. Capitalism, baby.

Kellogg's had other reasons for winding back the six-hour day – they were finding it harder to compete against other companies who stuck to the eight hours a day/40 hours a week work model. Fixed costs such as health insurance had also increased due to Kellogg's employing more people to work across four shifts instead of three. World War Two was the nail in the coffin, because it became harder to find enough people to cover the four six-hour shifts. Kellogg's gave a written guarantee that the reintroduction of the eight-hour work day was only for as long as the national emergency of the war lasted. Ha.

The company sought to divide the workers. It offered more senior workers more money to work longer hours, and divided men and women into different departments so six-hour days became seen as 'girls' work'. After years of this, the workers voted to return to the eight-hour day as the general rule. According to one woman who worked at the factory at the time, 'the work-hogs won'.

The bonus pay was done away with and the company was never able to achieve the production levels it obtained under it again.

According to historian Benjamin Kline Hunnicutt, management then acted 'in the fond hope that work would then blossom as the most rewarding aspect of life'. It turned to human relations, trying to sell to workers the idea that work done with the right attitude and proper expectations could be satisfying in and of itself. It's a microcosm of how 'work as the centre of your life' began to develop. Is work the centre of your life? Congratulations, you've been tricked by capitalism, like the rest of us.

It is interesting that the system in which we currently live in the western world has basically been set up to minimise all of the things science has proven over and over again make us happy – being outdoors, time with people we love, movement, etc., etc.

By 'interesting', of course, I mean 'depressing'.

There were still holdouts to ending Kellogg's six-hour work days completely, after the 'work-hogs' had won. A group of mostly women continued with their six-hour work days into the 1970s and it was finally abolished in 1984.

As Hunnicutt wrote in the *Business History Review* in 1992, the idea of virtue and happiness in working hard had well and truly solidified by then:

Instead of viewing human progress as transcending work, necessity, and economic concerns ... much of the industrial world shares the belief that work is an end in itself, the ultimate measure of progress and the definition of prosperity. Capitalists, managers and labor leaders have ceased dreaming of further work reduction and of 'necessity's obsolescence', pining instead for a world full of enough work for everyone or brooding about the 'work famine' to come.

If your basic needs are still met, a wage reduction should not matter much. If you want more leisure time, to be free, then the price of that will be reduced ability to buy things.

We only think we need to work full-time because we have been convinced by corporations in a bad system that we need to work full-time. Why do you think you need to work full-time? To afford everything? What is everything? How much of your consumption is things you actually need? You are mostly buying things you only think you need because you've been deluded by a broken system into thinking you need them.

Work has been so glorified that there are people who think they would do it even if they did not need to. You're a heretic if you don't have a life that is centred around work. People who say they would keep working if they won the lottery cannot imagine a life that is not completely organised around work.

The glorification of work has seeped into all other aspects of our lives, so there's a need to feel productive in almost everything that we do. Days off are to-do lists to be ticked off; hobbies are turned into side hustles, jogging into half-marathons and basic chores into 'life hacks'.

I am not above or cured of any of this. When I was in labour with my first son, I was still sending notes about my novel until the editor realised I was literally delivering my baby and told me to stop working.

I have always not only liked my jobs, but loved them. Well, the jobs after I stopped waitressing and working the supermarket checkouts. I really do believe journalism is important and therefore my small roles – reporting in Queensland, briefly in the press gallery, in Sydney as an editor – have contributed something to society. I have been so consumed by my work that I ignored my family, been unable to see friends, and talked only of the office and my tasks once on the couch in the evening with the person I love most in the world. Exhausted and overwhelmed, I still have a tendency to overwork. I know I could be having long lunches, swimming in the ocean, passing the time in a pleasurable way, but still I work.

***

We live in a society that is very individualistic. We spend a lot of time being the protagonist of reality, making ourselves bigger, whether it is through how we frame our lives on social media or what we project to the world on a daily basis.

We want to be useful. We want to be remembered. We think it's important to be important. But feeling insignificant can be such a comfort. There are reminders that we don't matter everywhere. Any time you have to wait in line for something; when a restaurant isn't able to book you in for your preferred time; when you look at the ocean and how enormous it is. It's all reminders of your insignificance, and, instead of feeling offended, it can bring relief. It is hugely freeing to know that how you spend your time only really matters to you. That you're not actually accountable to many people. That you can be swallowed up by many things more beautiful and mysterious. If you are busy looking at the world instead of within yourself, there are many chances to be awed.

As isolation progressed, my routine started to look like this:

7 am: Wake up and scroll the latest news.

7.30 am: Have breakfast delivered to me in the living room by my husband and the toddler while I begin work for the day.

8.57 am: Put on a bra and shirt.

9 am: Video news conference followed by hours of emails and phone calls and editing.

12 pm: Sandwich brought to me at my desk followed by hours of emails and phone calls and editing.

3–4 pm: Chase husband around the house. Ask him for hugs. Ask him what's on his computer screen. Ask him what he's thinking about. Ask for more hugs.

4–5 pm: Mad rush of work before picking up toddler.

5–6 pm: Work while ignoring confused toddler.

6–8 pm: Dinner with son, dance with son, yoga with son, reading with son, argue about having a bath with son, argue about going to sleep with son, put son to sleep.

8–11 pm: Dread.

Gradually I found how easily I could make the days on the weekend disappear. I would intend to have a shower at 10 am and read a couple more pages of a book, wipe down a table, do a drawing with my son, and then it was 5.30 pm and I was still intending to have a shower. If I didn't plan it, if I didn't worry about it, it was easy to let the hours pass me by, and it was fine that I was not achieving anything.

The actor Ellen Burstyn has what she calls 'should-less' days. Days off when there is nothing she 'should' do. She watches some television. She takes a nap. She does what she wants. My dread never fully abated on my own should-less days, but it was very gently incorporated so it was easier to withstand.

***

It seems so radical and so twee at the same time to say that it actually sucks to be your best self.

One of the joys to be rediscovered is the joy of being unproductive – leisure for leisure's sake. Instead of the latest bestselling non-fiction and Yoga with Adriene videos, there is spending Saturday the way you actually want to: reading a Meg Wolitzer novel from ten years ago and eating chocolate. In a time when we make sure we watch all the TV shows everyone is talking about, consume the long reads, do at least 10,000 steps, we could simply be doing what we want, without updating anyone on where or why.

Easy to suggest, harder to implement. I am still someone impressed by status, even though I am trying very hard not to be. I am still very ambitious – I wrote this book on maternity leave from my real, demanding job! I am desperate for people to know I was here and for it to mean something. Even though I know where and when I am truly happy – which is not at work or on television or when I hold a book I wrote in my hands – I still strive.

I don't think your life has to have grand ambition or even a purpose. It is fine to wander around finding interesting things until you die. People are looking for a big lightning strike, the one thing that will make sense of their life. But really what we have is a series of small realisations.

Life is made up of small decisions every day and a few big ones. You choose to live in a smaller place closer to the city or a bigger place further away from fun. You choose to make more money or have more free time. You choose to do a job you enjoy or one that is more boring but is going to give you the lifestyle you want. Children or no children. Monogamy and security or excitement and loneliness. A cooler city or your lifelong friends. Being thin or being satisfied. Being happy where you are or risking something different.

The big decisions and the small ones all form a perception of yourself. The early 30s are a big reckoning for people who define themselves by their job. Who define themselves by achievements, domestic or professional. It is a reckoning that the thing outside of yourself is not the thing that can make you happy.

Are you a mother or are you someone who has kids? Are you a writer or are you someone who writes? Are you a bad person or are you someone who sometimes does bad things? How you see yourself forms the big questions and each day brings all the small decisions.

The impulse to extract some small meaning from my life with a checklist has not dissipated. I cannot just vanquish it with rational thoughts, but I can try to take delight from the things I couldn't be bothered to do.

There's a lot to be said for wasting time, for being satisfied with passing the time in a pleasant way instead of worrying about what you're achieving. Each day you can work on the novel or not. You can read six books to your kid or not. You can cook a lovely dinner or order hot chips. You can make the bed or not.

It's OK to not achieve anything.

Travel will not make you a better person

Travel, we are told, is an exceptional way to expand the mind. Want to learn more about other cultures? Travel. Want to have an epiphany? Travel. Want to learn something about yourself? Travel. Want to be a better, more well-rounded person? Travel travel travel.

The result of this is hearing the same experience told by various 20-something-year-old men in different pubs across your city.

'On a boat in Croatia I ...'

'At the running of the bulls I ...'

'In a little bar in New Orleans I ...'

'Somewhere in Vietnam on a motorbike I ...'

Truly, it is kind of extraordinary how many people of a certain class and age have been to the exact same places. Berlin, Bali, Portland, Tokyo, Rome, Paris, the list goes on.

For a lot of people it starts with a circuit of Europe straight after school, backpacking between hostels or Airbnbs depending on budgets, and progresses to parts of Southeast Asia, before graduating to a couple of holidays that usually involve New York at some point, another lap of Europe in nicer hotels, a month spent in a few countries in South America, and Bali or Fiji at various life stages.

Very nice if you can afford it.

Even when people talk about being 'broke' while backpacking in their early 20s, they had enough security to be able to return when they ran out of funds. They had a home they could live in rent free usually, and money earned from shitty jobs could be put towards paying off debts rather than, say, living week to week.

Going 'broke' while backpacking was unthinkable when I was at university. Going into debt for anything other than an electricity bill or a rental bond was not possible on my planet, and moving back home would've meant moving three hours away from my university, which I was able to go to because I was on scholarship but therefore could not take a semester off. It would've been too many backwards steps. My parents did not have the money to pay my rent; it was something I had to do from the week I landed on the Gold Coast when I was 18.

Besides, my bedroom had been taken over by one of my many siblings within about 12 hours of me moving out.

I bought into the mythologising around travel, though. I understood that there was something meaningful about 'seeing the world'. Meaningful for myself, but also meaningful for other people's perceptions of me. It was something you could say about yourself without saying much, really. I started working full-time when I was 22, slowly started to become secure, and was able to become the type of person who 'travelled'.

In the past 10 years, the imperative to travel has been put through the Instagram lens. Now we can see where everyone else is going and the hell of a time they are having. Usually it's framed as a hell of a *good* time and countries get flattened into a brightly coloured wall here and a few appealing plates and cocktails captured from above there. Instagram may not influence the country you visit – although it can – but it will almost certainly influence the types of activities you do there. 'Doing it for the 'gram', a catchcry meant in irony, becomes literal when someone is on their holiday. Many people are in the perpetual state of framing potential photo opportunities and running through pithy captions as they walk the streets of Paris, roam a gallery in Barcelona and even 'relax' by the infinity pool at the resort. The time it *looks* like they're having is as important as the time they are actually having.

***

I soon realised that what people were often talking about when they 'travelled', and what I was doing when I 'travelled', was actually going on holiday.

Most people who have 'travelled' Europe and Asia and South America, basically anywhere, have usually just gone on holiday a lot.

Which is fine! And very fun. And sometimes very tedious. But 'going on holiday' has been infused with romantic ideals about doing something more noble than what it actually is.

To be 'seeing the world' and 'learning about other cultures', you also have to do the right kind of travel. The snobbishness around cruises is all the evidence you need for that. I cringe when one of my peers rolls their eyes at another news story about a cruise ship, or when someone jokes about people deserving what they get if they go on cruises when some minor disaster hits, like a gastro outbreak.

These same people think it's important to see the world, but if you are doing it in a way that is comfortable for you, or with the wrong kind of people, then you are failing at 'travelling'. Yes, you can even go on holiday in a way that can be sneered at.

As the coronavirus spread in the first three months of 2020, cruise ships became floating plague ships in the public imagination. One case on a ship would soon turn into 100 and ships were denied docking at various ports or forced to shut their passengers in their cabins. In Australia, the *Ruby Princess* became shorthand for the virus's spread across the country. More than 600 cases were eventually linked to the cruise ship, which had taken a scenic trip to New Zealand and back. In the *Sunday Telegraph*, I read of the passengers who had died. A man who had decided to join his partner of 30 years and her friends on the cruise. A woman on a reunion trip remembered for being 'a good dose of fun'. A woman who celebrated her birthday on the ship and then died in hospital as her husband lay ill next to her.

As the *Ruby Princess* passengers began to solidify the seriousness of COVID-19 for Australians, people were beginning to flee home. Home from overseas trips and home from living abroad. The decision had to be made quickly. Do you want to face the global health pandemic in London or Australia? New York or Australia? As thousands of millennials chose home, the borders began closing, and our 'options being sealed off' became literal, not just a turn of phrase.

For years, travelling and living overseas in your 20s and 30s was regular, another rite of passage. And now it is not.

Travel has radically changed and democratised since the 1960s and now it has been radically changed again, in ways we are still grappling with. It will be years before people can move that freely around the globe again, years more before many people can afford to. People not only found themselves stuck in the confines of the country they live in, but in their own city, in their own suburb. What do we do now that we cannot travel?

***

My youngest sister, Alice, had dreamed of going to Europe since she was a child. All through her teen years there were aspirations of … well, I'm not exactly sure. Vague pictures of the Eiffel Tower and pasta in Italy, probably. As she entered her early 20s, financial realities kept her from those dreams, but she still talked about it incessantly. My other sister, Anna, got a redundancy payout and very generously booked Alice her tickets. In a fever, Alice planned a trip taking in Morocco, France and Italy. The anticipation was contagious.

Finally on her dream trip, she wrote me an email:

Don't want to sound like a baby, I'm enjoying myself but I'd be happy to stay in the one country as well. I could just cry Bridie, been feeling like it since I've started the Europe adventure to be honest. Everyone thinks you have the best time travelling cause of social media but they don't realise the behind the scenes. I'll have an amazing time, I'm sure I will. I've got everyone praying [for me to be safe and enjoy myself]. I love seeing all the different places but still feels so surreal I'm here and I didn't think I'd miss you guys as much as I did and being close to home. Knowing I'm on the other side of the world. I'll really feel it when Pablo [a nickname for my first child, Hamish, who I was days away from giving birth to] is born but I'll solider on B, I'll be fine. It's all a learning experience. Love you. I had pasta today, and it was to die for.

I laughed and responded: 'Travelling does suck a bit, yes.'

There are the airports, and the waiting, and the heavy suitcase, and the unfamiliar, and the underwhelming food, and the dirty streets, and the parks that are not quite as nice as home. And the airports. Alice drank a lot of wine and met a lot of interesting people, just like how in Australia she drinks a lot of wine and meets a lot of interesting people.

She had learned the truth: if you want to expand your mind, if you want to learn something about yourself, you have to do something other than just go on holiday.

I think what had made my sister think that something more profound would happen was media – social and otherwise – telling us something more profound would happen. But also the fact that something very profound did actually happen to us when we travelled when she was a child.

***

My family did not take holidays. There were six to seven of us at different stages and my parents worked shift work in nursing jobs. The logistics and cost of holidays meant that they did not happen. During our school holidays we usually stayed at home, as did most people we knew in our country town. If people from our town did go on holidays, they went to one of the beaches within a 30-minute to three-hour drive from us. Even though I have now been going on holidays for years, it is still a novelty and each time I cannot quite believe it.

When I was 14, my granny was dying. She was in her 80s, the adored matriarch of our family, and was also in Derry, Northern Ireland, where she had raised my mother. This was very difficult for my mother, who was not in Derry, but in Grafton, Australia, where she was raising four children who, to her sometimes disgust and distress, behaved in a very 'Australian' way (according to her). 'Behaving like an Australian' could include but was not limited to: speaking back to Mum, ignoring Mum, forgetting to tell Mum something, telling her when we didn't like something and didn't want it, telling her when we did like something and did want it, and simply being annoying.

When staff at the hospital in Derry rang Mum to tell her that her mother was about to die, Mum responded: 'No she's not, she would've told me.' More than a decade before, Mum had made Granny promise her that Granny would tell her before she died. That she wouldn't do it suddenly while Mum was on the other side of the world. Mum got a nurse to hold up the phone to Granny, who I believe was unconscious or semi-conscious in bed. 'Mammy,' she said. 'I'm coming home.'

Mum had taken us to Derry once before when Alice was a baby, Anna was three, Séamus four and myself six to meet her sisters and brothers and see her mother, whom I had already met when she flew to Australia for my birth. Having raised ten children herself, Granny had sat in the kitchen and reassured my anxious mother that she was doing a fine job with her first baby.

This time, Mum would travel to Derry with her four children while Dad remained in Australia because he had to work and also because – I cannot emphasise this enough – my parents really, really did not like each other. Mum said she would be gone for a few weeks, and Dad waved goodbye to us at the airport.

When the few weeks were up, Mum phoned Dad and told him she couldn't leave. I can only speculate but I believe Dad would have understood how difficult it was for my mother to leave knowing that she would never see her mammy again. She could not return to Australia and fly home a second time, and Granny was very ill.

Mum found a house, moved Granny out of her assisted living home and into the house Mum had rented for all of us, enrolled us in school and that's how we ended up living in Derry.

It was 2002; the Good Friday Agreement, which ended most of the violence of the Troubles, had been signed only four years before. Derry is a small town. It's so small that when I was back there in my 20s, the first man shot in the Bloody Sunday massacre in 1972 bought me a beer at a pub my uncle hangs out in. That's how much the history of the city is a living, breathing thing – historical footnotes still walk around day-to-day buying groceries and going to the pub for a pint. The peace process is exactly that – a process. Peace is not just declared and then happens; people have to get used to it. Derry has changed a lot since then, but in 2002 it was still getting used to peace.

People like to claim and exaggerate their Irishness in Australia, but I was raised by an Irish woman who grew up in a war. Who left because the violence was too much to keep bearing witness to. Who moved across the world to have her babies away from bombs and everyone she loves the most in the world. I was not parented in the same way most of my classmates were. Philomena is loving to the point of suffocation, and expects a lot from her children. This has mostly been good for us, but she can sometimes seem quite mad.

In Derry in 2002, there was still a lot of sectarianism, there were still bomb scares. Séamus and I got used to being asked our religion, and if our Catholicism was inferred from our first names, we would offer our accents and Lebanese surname as proof of our observer rather than participant status. (When my brother returned a few years later, he would be kicked out of a party by someone yelling, 'Who brought this Fenian into my home?' after he learned the guy with an Australian accent was called Séamus.)

I never thought of Derry as a rough place, but it was still shocking to a 14-year-old from country New South Wales.

Séamus and I went to school in a Catholic enclave called Top of the Hill, in a predominantly Protestant area. In the 1970s, five men in their 20s to 50s were shot dead as they sat in a Top of the Hill pub watching the football. Nobody was ever prosecuted for the murders. Many street corners in Derry have that kind of story.

At lunchtime, we used to go outside of the school gates and throw rocks at the armoured police. We learned IRA chants – which my mother hated – and I smoked cigarettes for the first time on the 400-year-old walls with cannons built in to 'protect' the English and Scottish settlers.

There were times late at night, when I was out and shouldn't have been, that I felt terror for the first time in my naive life, though that terror was more about being out late at night when my mother thought I was asleep in bed.

It was so much fun. Ridiculously fun. The violent history felt close enough to be thrilling, but still abstract enough to be nothing worse than thrilling.

I have a huge, loving and hilarious family in Ireland that I feel very close to; it feels like home. But it was a home I got to come home from.

My siblings and I returned changed people, in the unexplainable and profound way that is usually how travel is sold. We had learned an unholy truth about how badly people can treat each other, how much people can cling to futile violence, and what it's like to say goodbye to people you love and not know when you will see them again. We watched my mother say goodbye to her mother, knowing she would not see her again. My mum was in her 40s, old enough at the time for us to think she didn't need a mother anymore; now it is devastating to comprehend flying to the other side of the world away from your mother, knowing she would die, so your kids could continue their lives somewhere else.

I got to come back to my country New South Wales town at 14 years old with tales of going clubbing regularly, kissing boys and a Republican paramilitary so fierce they almost murdered the English prime minister once upon a time.

It was a clichéd travel story in that I would've been a very different person if I hadn't done it. It gave my siblings and I a deep love for Australia, a gratefulness we shared with my Lebanese paternal grandfather, because we had seen close up what the alternative was.

But at 14, it didn't occur to me that my freedom from sectarianism and English colonialism had come at a very heavy price for the people who were actually from Australia. That reckoning would come later.

Because I was in country New South Wales, it was years before I even knew Australia was a place I was supposed to be embarrassed about.

***

There is a history I would later learn to be furious about and there are certainly parts I feel ashamed of, but I have never been embarrassed of Australia. It wasn't until I moved to Sydney that I met all the comfortable people who were embarrassed to be from here as they looked longingly to London or New York. I suppose I should have some cringe that my cultural education was so lacking that I didn't even know what 'cultural cringe' was until my mid-20s.

Originally coined by A A Phillips in 1950, the term 'cultural cringe' is used to describe a feeling of inferiority to other cultures (usually English or American). Since then, the phrase has spread to countries as varied as Nigeria, Canada, India and New Zealand. In Brazil, it is called the 'mongrel complex'.

Muhammed Badamasi wrote for *YourCommonwealth*:

In Nigeria, cultural cringe has gradually become synonymous with best practice. There is a general belief held by many Nigerians that whatever is Nigerian is naturally inferior to its western counterpart. At the same time, whatever is not

184

Nigerian is best practice ... The effects of colonialism and neo-colonialism are to blame for cultural cringe. Our traditions and cultures were consciously replaced with foreign ones by the colonialists, our values were decried and our way of life regarded as second rate. This instilled a feeling of inferiority which has been passed down from generation to generation, consciously or unconsciously.

When I told author and Aboriginal woman of Goorie and European heritage Melissa Lucashenko that I was writing about cultural cringe in Australia, her immediate reaction was there was not *enough* cultural cringe here.

'Or it's got the wrong cultural cringe in that there's so little understanding of the original Australian cultures that the settler culture doesn't even know,' she told me.

'The vastness of the ignorance is such that this society doesn't even understand its own inadequacy. And there's some good things about mainstream or white, [or] rather settler Australian culture. Those good things would include having some allegiance to egalitarianism, although I think that's fading, and that's probably the main thing I can think of.

'Australia has spent two centuries, you know, thinking of itself as vaguely inferior to the UK and the US and continental Europe without understanding that they've come in and trampled upon a culture that took

100,000 years to evolve and create, and the treasures of that culture are still invisible to Australia.'

We had such a neat illustration of this recently that it seemed as if it had been workshopped for a script. On 24 May 2019, the mining company Rio Tinto blew up the Juukan Gorge caves. Rio Tinto packed the caves with 66 tonnes of explosives with the full knowledge that they were a sacred site for the the Puutu Kunti Kurrama and Pinikura peoples. A sacred site that was 46,000 years old. The caves had been sitting there for more than 40,000 years before Jesus was even thought of. The oldest pyramid in the world is estimated to have been built about 5000 years ago. Stonehenge, described as a 'British cultural icon', is about the same age. Notre-Dame, which triggered an outpouring of grief worldwide when the cathedral was partially destroyed by fire, began to be built about 900 years ago.

Before Rio Tinto blew up the caves, it retrieved a few 'artefacts', including a 4000-year-old belt of plaited human hair that shows a direct genetic link to modern-day Puutu Kunti Kurrama and Pinikura peoples. The CEO resigned over the disaster – and it is the dictionary definition of a disaster – but the caves are gone. It was done to pursue an additional $134 million in high-grade iron ore.

The disrespect should take your breath away, but I don't think it came as a huge surprise to many of the Aboriginal and Torres Strait Islander people in Australia. The cultural cringe I regularly witness isn't about this, though. It's got nothing to do with the rich history of our First Nation people and everything to do with thinking that people in Australia are not very smart, from the average person in Far North Queensland to the people who populate our media class.

* * *

You can afford to think things are far superior overseas if you went to the right kind of school, and have the right kind of skin colour. It's an attitude that has pervaded Australia since quite soon after invasion. In other places, they have a rich intellectual culture. In other places, their politics are more refined. Even, in other places, they wouldn't consider making a dinner reservation before 9 pm. There is not much consideration for all the other places where they are having a far worse time.

Australian Jill Kerr Conway, who did eventually move to America, wrote in her 1989 memoir *The Road to Coorain* about the tendency of our academics and 20-something-year-olds to always be looking towards England as the pinnacle of refined society; and of the failure to see what was right in front of us, our own cultural traditions, and this country's long, long history.

'I loved its medieval and early modern history and detested its imperial complacency,' she wrote of England.

Just as England spectacularly fails to reckon with its colonial bloodbath, Australia is not very good at talking about the truth of how most of us came to be here.

Can settler Australians be proud of Indigenous history, however, given that, as Lucashenko pointed out, they are the ones who have trampled all over it?

'We don't actually know much about pre-European history, but we know a lot about pre-European cultures,' she says.

'Can they [settler Australians] be proud of it? I'd say they can learn about it. And they should. They should learn about it and try to understand it. I don't know about pride; cultural pride is tricky for all people because it has some echoes of fascism for me. [Indigenous culture is] to be understood, it's to be embraced, it's to be marvelled at. But because nobody alive today played a part in creating that, I don't know about pride.'

This does not mean Lucashenko agrees with me that the benefits of travel have been overblown. She thinks there is value in travelling overseas, and value in travelling across Australia, as long as we are invited and welcomed by the communities we are travelling to.

'There's a line in a song by John Gorka that says something like, "we can learn most from the people who aren't like us". And that's obviously a truism when you think about it. But we need to leave our homes and leave our families intellectually to learn, and probably emotionally as well.'

***

Since the 1980s, our eyes have partly turned from England and towards the USA. New York especially is revered by some as the pinnacle of rigorous thought and vibrant cultural life.

One of my friends recently forwarded me an article from a prominent press gallery journalist with the comment, 'It is miserable what passes for intellectual rigour here. Once again Australia showing its ass to the world, what an insignificant ...' Blah, blah, I tuned out. This friend is always moaning about how terrible our commentators are, often saying something along the lines of 'this would never be published in America' or 'if this was published in America, this writer would be laughed out of the country'.

Sure, I thought, the piece my friend sent me is not good, but have you been reading the news? The USA is not an egalitarian, thinking man's paradise.

It confounds me that people can look to a country where in some states teachers live on food stamps, where an inadequate health system only serves those who can afford it (something I consider inhumane and unforgivable), and can put all of that aside for a cerebral, writerly, New York Public Library fantasy.

I guess people like that only have the intellectual life to consider. There is plenty I find intellectually stimulating here.

I have a friend who talks of the need to 'breathe' as the reason for why she travels. She says she can feel claustrophobic in Melbourne where everyone knows her name and she knows what is around every corner. She says she sometimes needs to escape the parochial attitudes and small-mindedness of Australians.

Ah, I joke to her, by going somewhere where racism doesn't exist, such as … France.

When you are escaping the parochial attitudes of your home, it is just to another place with parochial people whose attitudes you didn't grow up with.

In 2014 I visited Beirut with my boyfriend, curious about the place I had sort of come from. I was stunned by the city. By the vibrancy, and ruins that had been around at the same time as Jesus, and temple complexes that took 300 years to build with stones weighing many tonnes pushed uphill somehow (like the pyramids, we do not know how) and bars with at least six languages being spoken in them at any one time, and cafés spilling onto the footpath at midnight with families eating charcoal-seared meats and young people arguing about Middle Eastern politics and Disney movies. By day I swam in the warm clear Mediterranean and thought, 'This place has it all.'

The Syrian war was raging at the time and the Australian government had issued 'do not travel' warnings for areas in the north, south and east of the country. Being the joyously indestructible 25-year-old that I was, I found a Lebanese woman who was still taking tours to Baalbek in the east. To get there, we drove through checkpoints manned by soldiers with huge guns (I don't know what type) and past kilometres and kilometres of refugee camps – towns made out of sheets with no running water housing the 1 million who had so far fled over the mountain that was the border with Syria. In Baalbek, I could have jogged to Syria within about 25 minutes. Watching the endless camps stream past our car windows, my chest hurt at the horror.

With the bleeding heart I had inherited from my mother, and much to the chagrin of my boyfriend, I gave my money to any child on the streets who asked for it.

The woman taking us to Baalbek was about 45 years old and, like a lot of Lebanese, spoke Arabic, French and English. After considering the camps for about five kilometres, she turned to us and said: 'This has been so terrible for us.'

I nodded. Nothing in my small life compared.

She continued: 'They come here and we just let them! They claim it's so hard for them back in Syria but then they jump on a plane out of Beirut and go on to some country in Europe they think will be better. Every year I holiday in Greece and I cannot go this year because the flights are so expensive because of all these Syrians claiming they are refugees, but they've got plenty of money.' She believed the Syrian refugees were taking her holiday seats to Greece.

In Hawaii a few years later, I got talking to a Black taxi driver about his country's first Black president, born in Hawaii. He looked at me sideways. 'That n**ger ain't born here,' he said. A few hours later, another Black man in a karaoke bar in downtown Honolulu told me that Barack Obama was born in Nigeria.

I turned to the bartender. What did she think? Was Obama born here? She shook her head and went back to pouring beers.

Isn't it funny how home can follow you wherever you are.

I tell these stories not to say, 'See, look, it's not just confined to Australia! We can all be small-minded!', but to observe that there is no escape from small-mindedness and parochialism, no matter where we go. There are people who are smarter than you everywhere. There are people who are more narrow-minded than you everywhere.

There is no place that does not need fixing. There are desperate people everywhere. There are privileged racist people everywhere. There are people who don't know whether they will live to the end of the week and there are people who whinge about running out of coffee beans on a Saturday morning (me).

Even while being aware that travel has been turned into another way for us to consume and another box to tick on our way to being interesting, productive people, I still managed to drop what I've learned while travelling. I hope you enjoyed that. It's not that I think people shouldn't travel, or that it isn't fun, or that it is pointless. It's just laden with far more meaning and sold with an idea of more originality than the reality of it. Like weddings. Or turning 30.

***

If travel is not for broadening the metaphorical horizons, along with the physical ones, then what is? How do you become the person you're supposed to be? Or a person in the world who's OK with your triviality? Or someone learned about the world? Especially now we may not even get the chance to travel.

If you are someone who gets a lot out of travel, then you are likely someone who is already open to the world. Open to learning, open to extraordinary things. It is not travel that is changing you, or opening your eyes, but your willingness to be moved. You'll have that whether or not you travel to Moscow or Alaska. Whether you have gazed at a Rousseau post-Impressionist painting in real life or seen the cherry blossoms bloom at Osaka Castle. If you allow yourself to be moved, then you can be moved wherever you are.

At the end of my street is a café run by an eccentric older man who supports Liverpool FC. I know this because there are about 30 signs in the café supporting Liverpool, and a bike parked inside next to a sign saying, 'parking for

Liverpool fans only'. He, or someone close enough to him to be allowed to hang things on the wall, has written out quotes in black marker on paper bags. I am not sure if they are meant to be uplifting: 'Only a fool ducks when the truth is thrown at him.' 'Damaged people are dangerous. They know they can survive.' 'In the end promises are just words.'

He is pretty quick at making coffees but spends twice as long perfecting babyccinos. He puts in two marshmallows. He covers it in chocolate. He gives it to the child for free. He also keeps biscuits with M&Ms on them on the counter, which he hands out to all children, also for free. I don't think I have ever seen him ask a parent if it is OK to give their child the biscuit. I don't think it has ever occurred to him to ask. He chats quite easily to my son, but always seems surprised when I try to strike up a conversation with him. I think he is extraordinary.

The other night I caught an Uber. The driver had a silver beard and I guessed him to be in his 60s. He seemed happy to pick me up. During the course of a casual conversation, he told me there was about ten years between his eldest and the next three children.

'Oh,' I laughed. 'You were almost independent and you started with the nappies all over again.'

Never, ever joke about big age gaps between siblings.

'It wasn't quite like that,' he said, hesitating. 'When my oldest was just under two years old, his babysitter left him in a car and they found a box of matches.'

The babysitter came out of the place she was in to see two men dousing the car with water, which had been entirely engulfed in flames.

'Where are the children?' she screamed.

'What children?' the two men asked. They had not seen the three children in the back seat through the flames.

His son was with two other boys, aged two and a half and four. Those two boys died. His son spent every night of his next four years in hospital.

He told me what it was like. What it was like to be at the hospital next to his burned son every day for four years. What it was like to watch him grow up. What it was like to help him carry on with life. What it was like to watch one of the other boys die in hospital.

I just tried not to cry too much. He was a lovely man, and an extraordinary father.

Sometimes when I am catching the train in the city, I look up and see Sydney Harbour sparkling in front of me, with glorious blue sky underneath the man-made feat that is the Sydney Harbour Bridge. It can be blue like my brother's eyes. Blue like the river I grew up on, which I used to think was bottomless. Blue like something precious, a jewel worth a lot of money. And I think, what an extraordinary place I live in. What an extraordinary time we are living in. What extraordinary people I meet. Anywhere I go.

Does the way you were parented matter when you have sisters?

Most mornings, I gaze adoringly at my son, just like you do in your imagination pre-kids, and I wonder two things.

The first is what terrible thing is going to happen to balance out this bliss I surely do not deserve. The second is what he is going to hate about me.

My hypocrisy? My limited attention span? That I make him wear a hat?

Lately I have been comforted by a realisation that although my parents loom as the two largest figures in my life (figuratively; they are actually quite short people), when I look back upon my childhood they are relegated to supporting cast. They shimmer in the background of most of my memories like ghosts, which disappear if I try to look directly at them. I am sure they were there, but I can't quite place them most of the time.

I remember, when I was four years old, my dad turning ashen-faced as I ran to him from the backyard bleeding profusely from a deep gash next to my eye and him saying shakily, 'Go down to your mother.'

I remember, when I was a teenager, my mum standing on the verandah one night, ordering me back inside so she could yell at me. Because she was Irish, she was terrified of what creatures lurked in our Australian yard. Knowing full well she wouldn't venture any further, I stood in the dark only a few metres away, yelling back, 'No!'

But the rest of the time I remember my brother and sisters. Lighting fires in our secret spot in the shed. Hiding underneath the house at night while playing tag. Finding Alice hiding in my wardrobe, where she had been for 90 minutes, because she was so desperate to hang out with her cool teenage sister and her friend. Making up dances, making up songs, making up concerts, making up radio shows, making up our identities.

How much am I the person I am today because of my parents? And how much is because of my siblings? Was it my mother or my brother who made me the kind of person who easily bosses other people around? Was it my father or my sister who made me someone who incessantly asks questions to the point of irritation?

Did my brother make me assertive? Did my sister make me funny? Did my other sister make me short-tempered? Did my brother and sisters make me funny?

There are reams of studies about the effects of nature versus nurture, primarily focused on the influence of parenting styles upon their baby. There are scores of Facebook parenting groups where you can be scolded, judged and potentially vilified over simple domestic choices such as whether your baby was given formula or if you tell your kids Santa is real (apparently that is lying to them). Modern-day middle-class parents are obsessed with topics like what ages milestones such as talking and toilet training happen, how to create independent toddlers, and the Right and Wrong way to do things. Sometimes I think they are convinced they can be, if not a perfect parent, then objectively better than 90 per cent of the parents they know. I think that, beyond creating loving and secure environments, they overestimate their influence.

The influence of siblings upon character is a much more niche area of study.

A peer-reviewed article published in the *United States National Library of Medicine* found that between 1990 and 2011 there were 33,990 citations for 'parent or parenting' in abstracts of psychological and social studies. There were 8685 citations for 'marriage or marital relationship or marital relation', 5059 citations for 'peer relations or peer relationships or friendships' and just 741 citations for 'sibling and relation or relationships'.

It found sibling relationships to be very under-studied, but the evidence that was available pointed to siblings being a fundamental relationship that could teach people how to work with other people, argue (ha), problem-solve and influence things from how they responded to stress as an adult to what age they lost their virginity.

There is even a great body of evidence showing that siblings have a protective effect against hay fever, atopic eczema, allergic sensitisation and asthma, although it is not known what factors cause this.

Another study recognised four major characteristics in relationships between brothers and brothers, and brothers and sisters, and sisters and sisters. The first was how emotionally charged these relationships are and how uninhibitedly emotions are expressed, whether the relationships are positive or negative. It found that it was quite rare for a sibling relationship to be ambivalent.

When Séamus and I were about nine and eleven, we used to have ferocious physical fights. The four of us still talk about the most famous one in awed tones more than 20 years later. We rolled along the ground, moving from the bathroom to the hallway and eventually the living room, landing any punch we could until he ripped out a handful of my hair and I kicked him with all my strength in the balls. It was full of so much fury, our younger sisters followed us crying and screaming, 'You're going to kill each other! You're going to kill each other!'

The physicality of relations between my brother, my sisters and I was and still is a real hallmark. We would sit on top of each other while watching television, slap and hit each other, fall asleep in single beds hugging each other, wrestle, push each other off trampolines, tackle each other to the ground, kiss each other and play with each other's hair. Our childhood is a blur of tangled limbs.

The second characteristic of sibling relationships is intimacy. Long hours, long days, long years spent playing with each other, hanging out, doing not much near each other means you know each other inside out. According to the study, a long history and intimate knowledge means there are plenty of opportunities to provide support to each other, have conflict and understand each other's points of view.

For us, this intimacy has certainly moved into adulthood as we turn to each other in our happiest and toughest times. I lived with Anna for a year, she has lived with Alice for a few stretches, who lived with Séamus for a year, who has lived with me for months at a time at different points. We only have to say to each other, 'Don't tell anyone but …' and the other person will dissolve in laughter. If you are starting a sentence with 'Don't tell anyone but …', it means it won't be long until the entire family knows what you're about to say.

The third characteristic is the quality of relations with each other, while the fourth is the age difference, which, no matter how big or how small, often means issues of power, control, rivalry and jealousy, as well as teaching, helping and caregiving.

The study wryly observes that sibling relations can make parenting difficult, because parents cannot treat siblings all the same, but we definitely notice when parents treat us differently. When I was a kid, I was only allowed fruit and a Vita-Weat in my lunchbox as my snack, and I still bring up with Mum the fact that after I left home the others were allowed Roll-ups in their lunchboxes. Roll-ups! I begged for Roll-ups! NOT FAIR! Not mentioned in the study is how obsessed with fairness siblings are, and by fairness, I mean: what the other sibling has that I don't.

Liane Moriarty, the Australian author who became a global sensation, really told on herself when she revealed how she got started on her first book.

'I can still remember exactly where I was when I found out she'd got her first deal,' she told the *Sydney Morning Herald*, talking about her sister Jaclyn Moriarty. 'I feel like I can see the camera zooming in on me. I was in my office [as marketing manager for a legal publisher], with my shoulder pads, in North Ryde, thinking I was pretty good, and she rang. She was so excited. And I was excited for her. It seemed so amazing: that you could actually get published!

'And she's such a beautiful writer: she's never written a boring sentence in her life. But there was the other feeling – sheer rage! No, no – but definitely disappointment with myself, that I hadn't done it and she had.'

Within two years, Liane had written her first book

She saw her sister get something and she wanted it. I deeply relate.

Stories like that make it surprising to me that the influence of siblings could be such an understudied area. Your siblings are probably the longest relationship you will have in your life, they have to have a profound impact. But it is difficult to quantify – most sibling studies note that two siblings in the same family can have vastly different experiences of it.

It was actually an episode of *Keeping Up with the Kardashians* that made me recognise my bone-deep subjectivity in my intense relations with my sisters. Khloe and Kim had been so mean to their eldest sister, Kourtney, making sly comments and little digs that did not seem like much, and then acting surprised when she got angry or burst into tears. I recognised the cunningness instantly. It is one of my worst traits, occasionally saying seemingly innocuous things like, 'How old is that jumper?' in the full knowledge I am scratching a deep insecurity few know about. Casual cruelty followed by an innocent 'What?'

Kourtney was so upset, the scene ended with some serious violence. Kim, her hair perfectly done, slapped Kourtney as hard as she could, while Kourtney lashed out, scratching Kim's back and arm hard enough to draw blood.

As their mother said later, 'It hurt my soul to see my children acting like that at 39 and 40 years old.'

Forty years old and your sister can still provoke you into physical violence. Only sisters can understand.

A woman I know with five brothers sent the clip of the Kardashian sisters fighting to my group chat to talk about how fake it was, but I and two other women with sisters only had to watch it once.

'It's real,' we all wrote back.

In the aftermath, Khloe and Kim would talk about how it 'came out of nowhere' and how in the wrong Kourtney was. They could have been genuinely oblivious to their bullying of her. Their sister was having a completely different experience of the same family. Where they saw ambition and mutual support, Kourtney saw greed and intimidation.

Different experiences of the same environment have been a key part of the limited research into the impact of sibling relationships. One of the most influential articles on sibling research, 'Why are children in the same family different from each other', found it was 'not implausible' that parents of siblings had less influence on their children than parents with just one child.

It found that siblings' relationships with each other and their relationships with their friends likely had more impact on their personality than their parents treating them differently. The conclusion of the research, which unsettled the scientific community at the time, essentially found that two rich brothers who went to the same school and had parents who took them to the same cultural events, gave them the same books to read and had them play the same sports were no more similar to each other than they were to two boys from a poor family who grew up on a farm.

What shaped a person were the differences in their environments, not the similarities. The main differences could be parental treatment, how their brothers or sisters treated them, and their relationships with mates.

One parent cannot raise two children exactly the same, of course, especially if they are different in age, but trying to study if parents treat their children differently is a fraught process with a lot of personal bias. The researchers found that when they asked siblings if they were treated differently by their parents, most answered yes, but when they asked the parents, most answered no. This will surprise precisely nobody who has or has ever had a brother, a sister or both.

The closest we have to an objective finding is a longitudinal study of 50 families, which filmed a mother interacting with each of her two children when they were both one year old. The films were made roughly three years apart and looked at affections, verbal attention and control. It found that overall the mothers were 'remarkably consistent' and did not treat their children differently, a finding which has been replicated in other longitudinal studies.

The article found evidence that basically no shared

environmental influences made for similar behaviour traits, and what we are really formed by are all the things we experienced that were different. Such as each other.

Another longitudinal study into single-parent African-American families in rural areas found direct links between the eldest child and positive behavioural changes in their younger siblings over the years. Researchers have even suggested trialling programs to improve outcomes for at-risk youth by focusing on building the relationships with their siblings.

Basically, it matters a lot more what our brother or sister were like than whether your parents gave you wooden toys and paintbrushes or noisy plastic trucks and television. It was all about who you were playing with.

It is difficult, if not impossible, to trace the origins of many aspects of my personality. I have always thought of my brother and sisters and myself as proof of nature winning out in the nature-versus-nurture debate. We are all very close in age and somehow completely foreign to each other in a lot of ways. But what we all share, that we almost certainly got from each other, is a supreme self-confidence that comes from a fierce protection.

Most of the time we all think we are the most interesting people in a room. Not in an arrogant way, but in the way that happens when you have three other people who love you so much because of, and sometimes despite, the person you are.

OK, also in a little bit of an arrogant way. We find each other so interesting, how could the world not find us interesting?

Multiples studies have found that through fighting with your sibling when you are a child, you can develop skills in looking at situations from another perspective, negotiation and persuasion, and all of these skills are linked to emotional understanding and empathy as an adult.

When I was getting my little sisters to do what I wanted with threats that I wouldn't invite them to my birthday party if they didn't, or when I was flogging the shit out of my brother, we were learning how to be in the world as adults.

It's not all positive, however; if sibling influence can go one way, then it can almost certainly go the other. Sibling relationships have also been linked with bullying behaviour in teen years, school problems and even substance abuse. Older siblings in particular can provide models of 'deviant behaviour'. So I guess it's a good thing my younger siblings had such an exemplary role model in me. Another thing they can thank me for, along with the cash injections over the years.

Older siblings can even influence the way you are parented. A 2002 study found parents stressed much less about subsequent siblings' transition into teenagers after having already experienced the dizzying hormonal highs and lows of the firstborn. Even something as simple as their parents' altered expectations made for different parenting, especially combined with what parents learned from parenting the firstborn. Some studies have shown mothers and fathers are much more effective at parenting their younger children as teenagers, and have less conflict with them and higher levels of warmth. It could just be that the firstborn's teen years have exhausted them too much to be bothered by the second and third and even fourth time around.

It reminds me of an old joke: 'parents treat their oldest children like their first car: they write them off and then promise to do better with the next one'. My mother was probably giving my younger siblings Roll-ups in their lunches because she had realised it was not a fight worth having.

Your siblings can also help you decide who you *don't* want to be. There is scientific evidence that they can be your foil – someone you can compare yourself to and then act against, building yourself in contrast to them rather than in their likeness. Say you have a brash older sister, loud, imposing, in love with attention. You can build yourself into someone who doesn't have to be noticed, who can find her own interests and her own self while everyone is distracted by someone else.

It's not all overflowing with abundance of love and funny memories, though. Siblings bring their own specific claustrophobia, which is part of the reason you can be compelled to create your identity in opposition to them. This claustrophobia becomes extremely tedious as an adult. A seemingly innocent text can turn into a multi-week meltdown, inflaming old factional lines, roping in every family member.

My parents-in-law live in north Queensland and, after the birth of my second son, we had cancelled two trips for them to meet because of border closures. In October, with the border still shut, we booked a Hail Mary Christmas trip. My husband was working over Christmas, so we were going to be staying in Sydney anyway and his parents were able to take a rare four days off in a row from the pub they own. We had not seen them since the previous year.

I sent a text to my family group chat: 'Just booked Matt's parents to come here for Christmas, please light all the candles and say all the prayers that this one doesn't get cancelled like the last two.'

Within a minute, Anna, in Melbourne, sent a chilly response. Were they coming to Sydney or our hometown in northern NSW?

I live in Sydney, I responded.

And thus the fight began.

Anna said she thought we would all be in our hometown for Christmas since we hadn't been able to see each other much that year. I said that would've been nice, but Matt's parents hadn't seen us at all that year and Matt was working anyway. Séamus chimed in a with a simple 'I'm working Christmas' and Anna responded with a passive-aggressive, 'Great, I guess I'll see you in 2052'.

So I told her to fuck off.

Mum and Dad, who are both in the family group chat, remained silent.

In my last message, I said it was selfish of Anna to be mad that we were spending Christmas with Matt's parents. Alice responded an hour later with the iconic and baffling 'Anna is the least selfish out of all of us'.

The machinations of the family continued to grind along outside of the group chat, with Séamus privately sending Anna a message telling her to go easy on me and Dad privately sending me a message telling me not to get upset at my sisters.

We were already having our Christmas blue in October.

I tried to be mature and gave Anna a call that afternoon to clear the air. I said I was sorry I told her to fuck off and she said she understood why we were having Christmas in Sydney.

Then two hours later, the messages to Séamus began.

First Alice sent a series of messages going off at him for earlier telling Anna to look at things from my perspective. Then 30 minutes later came a long message from Anna about how Séamus was a terrible person for sending the message. When he didn't respond, she started sending another message every 15 minutes.

Since the dawn of time – well, since 1994 – our factions have roughly been Séamus and me versus Anna and Alice. If there are enough siblings for factions, then factions will exist. Like all factions, these can shift, and it doesn't actually mean we are closer to the person we are in the faction with, it's just old battlelines we revert to at times. We are all unreliable commentators on each other's actions, because usually I will back Séamus, he will back me, Anna will back Alice and Alice will back Anna, no matter what. So when I ask Séamus, 'Was I wrong to tell Anna to fuck off?', he will respond, 'Of course not, she needed to be told to fuck off.' Even though, really, it was wrong to tell Anna to fuck off.

By the next morning, there had been a phone call between Anna and Séamus in which any understanding between me and Anna had disintegrated and I was back to being selfish. Séamus was berated for not having Christmas off, even though he is one of 200 ICU nurses in one of the biggest trauma units in Australia and has to go into a ballot for that week off.

I truly am too old for this shit.

What the fight is really about, though, isn't Christmas. It's about feeling left behind when your sister has children. It's about who was Dad's favourite in 1998. It's about nostalgia. It's about the competition of who has it the toughest – the mother of a baby or the one in the longest and hardest second-wave COVID-19 lockdown in the world. It's about possessiveness and feeling second or third best. It's about the betrayal of someone you love getting married. It's about knowing someone your entire life.

***

Parenting matters, obviously. But so do a constellation of other people. Your friends, particularly when you're a teenager, can be the reason you decide to do a particular job, become political or become a stoner. A grandmother who thinks you are the singularly most marvellous person to have ever existed can give you an unshakeable foundation to build your self-esteem upon. Your brother or your sister will always be someone you can't dazzle, someone with whom you can't suppress the more unsavoury parts of your true self, someone who will know you your entire life. There will be things my sons will hate about me, for sure, but hopefully they will be thinking about each other too much to dwell upon them.

What are you defined by?

Here are some facts about me:

I am unconventional.

I am empathetic.

I am responsible.

I have a terrible temper.

I am a loose unit.

'Facts' may have been used too emphatically. They are descriptions of various aspects of my personality, by me. But are they actually by me? Is that what I am actually like? Or are they things other people have told me about myself and I believe them so then I act in an empathetic way, I behave responsibly, I get loose, as a kind of self-fulfilling prophecy?

When I began thinking about how people define themselves, *really* thinking about how people define themselves, I thought it was as straightforward as getting your identity from certain roles in your life. Work, or jobs, seemed like an easy thing people were defined by. Motherhood is another obvious one; over and over we see people consumed by it, seemingly unable to extract the individual from their child. Relationship status. Sexuality. It can seem a lot easier to define yourself by these things than to think too hard about the kind of person you are.

But, really, what so many of us are defined by is what other people think of us. We want them to think our life has meaning because we have children. We want them to think we are an interesting person because our job is interesting. It's quite difficult for a lot of people to conceive of themselves a certain way if nobody else thinks of them that way.

It's a galling realisation. Tied to what we define ourselves by is also what makes us happy, so does this mean that if my acquaintance doesn't think I am fun and smart, then I cannot be fun and smart? Is a crisis about our lives at 31 really a crisis about what other people think of us? What if we aren't actually who we think we are, but just behave in this way because when we were impressionable teenagers, adults told us we should be writers, or would not amount to much, or were very good at taking care of others?

Wrestle with these questions long enough and you can lure yourself into having an existential crisis. It's been proven in human behaviour again and again that so much of what we think is acceptable and appealing and exciting comes from what the people around us think is acceptable and appealing and exciting.

I have a friend, Fintan, who is the youngest of five children. As someone who was raised the eldest of five children, we can have some scary/funny insights into each other's psychology. He's a smart guy, a really smart guy, one of those people who, if you mention you went to Croatia, will tell you that when it was part of Yugoslavia the workers got free apartments and healthcare, but the apartments often did not have heating and it was difficult to get something as simple as antibiotics.

Once we were discussing a difficult local government zoning issue and he said offhandedly, 'But nobody really cares what I think, I'm quite dumb like that.'

For a moment I was shocked and then my eyes narrowed in recognition. 'Which sibling said that to you?' I asked.

He looked confused for a moment. 'What?'

'Who told you that you were dumb and nobody cared what you thought? The only person mean enough to say that is a sibling, and one of the only people who could say that to you and you would actually believe it is a sibling.'

Fintan started laughing. 'My older sister used to tell me that all the time.'

It was objectively not true, but here he was, at 38, deep down believing it about himself, because he was told he was dumb when he was young. Something that had been said to him had become a way he thought about himself.

Seeing yourself through other people's eyes can be as obvious as noticing you get more likes on Instagram when you post something funny about what a disaster your life is – people like you not-serious and admitting to fuck-ups! – or it can be as insidious as a teenage girl's comments 20 years before. It's not always a bad thing, but it can be terrifying to realise how much an offhand remark can be embedded in the consciousness of someone you love. Or even someone you barely know.

When I was 18, I overheard a conversation between my dad and someone else. When they asked if he was worried about me moving away, he replied, 'She's like her mother, she makes friends wherever she goes.' It is something I have used to self-soothe in stressful situations so much that it has become true. When I have moved cities, switched jobs, or even just gone to events where I don't know anyone, it has become a type of mantra on repeat: 'You'll be fine, you make friends wherever you go.' I very much doubt he even remembers saying it, and I have no idea if he still thinks it or how much he believed it at the time.

On a basic behavioural level, this is how trends happen. A few years ago, pastry chef and owner of Black Star Pastry in Newtown, Christopher Thé, created a cake with watermelon, two layers of almond dacquoise, rose-scented cream, strawberries, pistachios and dried rose petals. Soon there were lines down the block as people travelled from all over Sydney to taste it.

Then it took off on Chinese social media app WeChat and was dubbed 'the world's most Instagrammed cake'. Before long, people weren't travelling just across Sydney but across the globe to sample it; Black Star Pastry has even been designated a tourist destination by Destination NSW. There have been pop-up stores in different parts of Australia as well as other countries such as Singapore and Japan. In 2018, it was selling more than 16,000 slices a week.

The cake was a phenomenon. The cake is delicious and also photographs well, which was a big factor in its popularity on social media. It was also as simple as people saying it was good, and other people believing them. People lined up because other people had told them it was worth lining up for.

The same can be applied to your sense of self. We believe what other people think about us, more than some of us care to admit.

It can be quite difficult to figure out what you really think, and there's a danger that by the time you've figured that out you've already done the degree, started the career, moved to the city, because of what other people had said to you.

Eleanor Gordon-Smith, a philosopher in her late 20s at Princeton University, is (obviously, from that descriptor alone) a massive over-achiever. She is also someone who is averse to conflict. Or, at least, she thinks she is.

She often wonders what it would be like to wake up the next day and just behave in opposition to that 'fact' about herself.

'What if tomorrow I wake up and think, "Here's the thing that's defining about me: I'm actually really good at conflict. I'm not abashed, I'm not squeamish and not, like, too keen to make other people feel better." What if I just started behaving in a way that presumed that the other story was true? Would I be able to make it so it was true?'

It's why there is the temptation for so many to completely change their career, to travel, to move to the other side of the world. You don't have to be the same you if you're in a place where nobody knows you. The easiest way to change yourself is to change the people around you and therefore what people around you think of you.

It's impossible to get an objective answer from someone when you ask them to describe themselves. It's easy for someone to tell you they were told they were responsible when they were 12 and they still behave responsibly at 31, harder for someone to articulate the messages they were given that were not necessarily said out loud.

Eleanor agrees and even has an example that is terrifying for anyone who is a parent or, indeed, has a parent.

'An idea of yourself happens on a really subterranean level. One time your mum didn't put a picture up on the fridge even though you put hours and hours into drawing it, and so then you become convinced that your effort doesn't equal achievement and then that kind of becomes a self-reinforcing story and you look for evidence of that everywhere,' she says.

'It's not the kind of thing that you would agree with if someone described you that way or be in a hurry to say yourself. But I think if you dig deep enough, you can find that kind of thing.

'I really do think that so much of the way we define ourselves is as a result of the ways that we've been treated, and the things that people have reflected back to us about us. Not always intentionally. We are way more susceptible than we think to what other people reflect at us, about us.'

When I started thinking about how my life was turning out and what I wanted, what I didn't realise I was also thinking about was what other people thought of my life. Did I have enough admiration? I told myself I was having some kind of crisis about whether my job, my relationship, my family, my friends were actually making me happy. What I was actually concerned about was whether my job, my relationship, my family, my friends were admired enough by other people.

I had trouble separating my job from my sense of self, because it was a job a lot of other people found impressive, and also a job a lot of personal satisfaction can be extracted from. Which is a luxurious position to be in.

But if I am defined by my work, is there a possibility that people don't actually like *me*? That the only reason people like being friends with me is that it gives them proximity to the media, which they perceive to be powerful?

We don't get to form or exist in a vacuum. Of course it means something to us how much social reward and reinforcement we get for behaving in certain ways.

There are many, many people who are not defined by their jobs; it is simply the job they do. Eleanor says what more people are defined by, from a philosophical standpoint, is motivation.

'What is the goal? What's the thing that you want to leave behind? What's the kind of project that you want to achieve? A huge part of your sense of self comes from what you're working towards. And the reason I now think that is [because] once you stop having something to work towards, it's really easy to stop feeling like you have a sense of self,' she told me.

'I don't know how the mechanics of that work but I think [the purpose of] having goals, something that people get a lot of solace from, is it connects you to your future. To have a sense of self, you have to have a sense of continuity, you know, you have to have a sense that the thing that you are now is going to be in some way connected to the thing that you are tomorrow, the day after, and five years from now. And one way to get that kind of, like, javelin that moves forward into the future is to think in terms of projects, and think in terms of aspirations and goals. I think it does give us that way of connecting my current self to my future self, because they'll both be defined by their agreement that this project was worth doing. And that's kind of nice.'

It is wild that we set our lives up before we realise the person who we are. When you really think about it, it seems crazy that I picked a degree and a job at 18 that completely dictated where I would be living, the person I'd be in a relationship with and who my friends would be at 31. If it had been a catastrophic error, then how would I have known when to fix it?

You can't put those decisions on hold until you actually know who you are either.

I felt like grabbing every 82-year-old I could find by the shoulders and shaking them, asking, 'What age did you know who you are? Do I know now or am I still being fooled like I was at 18? Tell me!'

There are hardly any objective truths about anyone. When I say, 'Here are three facts about me,' I am absolutely talking some bullshit. I can't really say that I am empathetic as a fact; it is disingenuous to say it is I who gets to decide whether I am empathetic or not. But who knows me better than I do?

Instead, here are three factual stories about me.

***

Story number one: There is a woman I know who I'll call Annette. Annette has been beaten up multiple times by her partner. Each time she leaves him, she either sleeps on the streets or tries to get enough money from strangers to get a hostel for the night. I know this because she sometimes sits outside the Woolworths I pass on my way to work and she has a sign that explains the bare facts. We kind of got to know each other because whenever I saw her, I would go get $20 and give it to her and we would chat a bit. She's a pretty funny woman, obviously quite tough.

Once I went a few months without seeing her and tried to convince myself she had found some stable accommodation and that was the good-news reason she wasn't asking people for money in Surry Hills. Then one day I was walking through the CBD and saw her sitting on a corner with her head down. I had some notes in my wallet and went to give them to her. As I bent down, I realised she was crying. Crying and crying and crying. I also realised she had her leg out straight in front of her and crutches next to her. I asked her what was wrong.

'I just got out of hospital,' she said, still sobbing. She said something about being an idiot or being stupid. 'I went back to my boyfriend and he threw me down the stairs and he broke my leg and I've been in hospital for three months. I got out today and there's no room at the shelter for me, but I had to get out of the hospital. I couldn't be there any longer.' Annette was about to sleep rough, already a pretty

BRIDIE JABOUR

dangerous thing for a woman, and she couldn't run if she needed to. I could barely bring myself to think of how many times she might need to run.

'What are you going to do?' I asked.

'I can't stay at the hostel and the backpackers is $70 a night, but nobody will even look at me.'

I was stunned and I was furious. How many times had this woman been let down by our society? She had been released onto the street with nowhere to sleep and a broken leg.

I told her to wait where she was and went to an ATM and got out $200. When I came back, there was a woman who looked very inspired by Kim Kardashian. She had a long straight dark ponytail, an expensive leather handbag and a skirt suit that was a little short and very form-fitting. She even had on fake eyelashes for whatever office job she had. She was in her 20s and was kneeling down with her hand on Annette's shoulder, talking to her. I had a lot of love for this woman in that moment. A woman who wouldn't walk past a crying woman sitting on the ground.

I gave Annette the money and hoped it would get her through two nights at the backpackers, some good food, whatever she wanted.

'Are you serious?' she kept saying. 'Are you serious?'

I offered to help her up and walk her to the backpackers. 'Nah love, it's about lunchtime, I might get some more money sitting here.' She grinned.

'Hell yeah, Annette!'

I wrote down my mobile number and told her to call me if the shelter hadn't sorted anything out for her in the next couple of days. I felt virtuous and completely useless. That night I added the NSW Women's Shelter to my monthly donations.

I believe Annette and I believe she was using that money for a safe bed that night. But if she used it for anything else, whatever, it's her money to spend on whatever she needs to get through the day and night. It's not like I was going to spend the $200 on anything particularly noble.

***

Story number two: I own a $2000 handbag. I know it's an obscene amount to spend on a handbag and I have no justification for it. I love it.

***

Story number three: When my son was 15 months old, I went to a Mardi Gras party with some mates who will probably never know how much they boosted my self-esteem and confidence as I navigated the world as a 'mum'. Just the most beautiful, non-judgmental, joyous group of people.

Anyway, this is not an ode to them. I went to the Mardi Gras party and I got really, really high. Like *really* high. It was a very safe party and lots of people looked out for me. I blacked out and when I was aware of my surroundings again, my friend asked me who Lenore was.

Lenore? Why did they want to know about Lenore?

It was because when I was at my most incoherent, I was muttering to myself, 'I've just got to check it with Lenore. I'll see what Lenore thinks. I can't publish it until Lenore is OK with it.'

Lenore is my boss.

It turns out the thing deeply embedded in my consciousness, brought to the surface when I am at my most loose, is not the great human loves of my life, or my family, but work and what my boss thinks.

One of my mates had messaged my husband about how messed up I was when they were very worried I wasn't going to come out of it, and the next day he was understandably pretty cranky with me, because it's pretty annoying to be stressing about the stupid decisions of your 30-year-old wife at 2 am!

***

I don't know what you can tell about me from those stories. The first story can be read through a lens of white guilt, genuine compassion or even faux humbleness. The last can be very funny, or alarming, or the tale of a workaholic, or derogatory about the kind of parent I am. They are stories I am secretly very pleased with and secretly quite embarrassed about. I can't say what kind of person they make me.

It's hard to know what mantras I should take going forward with this information. I could be telling myself, 'Who cares who cares who cares' when getting tied in knots about how many right decisions I'm making. I could be more blasé. More dismissive. Work harder at being kinder. Try to separate myself from what other people think. Shut down all social media. I could even try therapy.

At the core of working out what defines you is a hell of a lot of thinking about yourself. This much self-reflection is a very modern phenomenon and, while it should not be breezily dismissed as self-obsession, it can easily veer into indulgent territory.

You can try to work out what defines you in order to determine how to lead a good life, how to get out of this existential rut, but you can also get so far stuck up your own ass mulling this stuff that you think you are the protagonist of life. Every cancelled train, every late food delivery, whether or not you are wasting this one precious and glorious life – it all matters because it is happening to you.

Me: 'Pretty much everyone has their own shit going on and I have to be considerate of that while also figuring out how to live a fulfilling and generous life.'

Me at even the most mild inconvenience: 'What the FUCK is this shit.'

Figuring out what defines you, how to live the best life, it's all in pursuit of having yourself explained to yourself. It's why we love personality tests like the Meyer-Briggs test, which has exploded in popularity among millennials in recent years outside of the usual corporate setting you are forced to take it in. It's why horoscopes are appealing and even the greatly exaggerated and often-cited extrovert/introvert binary. It feels neat to be able to say, 'I don't want to go to that party because I'm an introvert,' rather than simply, 'I don't want to go to that party.' People seem to describe themselves as introverts much more than extroverts because they think it explains something fundamental about them, when really most people don't always want to go to the party, most people like time out by themselves, most people often feel exhausted by other people. There is nothing wrong or particularly special about self-described introverts apart from 'the human condition'.

Whether you're The Artist or The Protector or The Mediator in the Meyers-Briggs, you're never going to be able to explain exactly why you are the way you are.

This is all stuff that makes up something important – your emotional hinterland. But it can also be part of something very unimportant – naval-gazing. Spend too much time gazing at your naval and you aren't going to find anything of value there, it just smells a bit funky.

***

To say Tyson Yunkaporta is an Aboriginal scholar really doesn't begin to cover what he is. He's a member of the Apalech Clan in Far North Queensland, a lecturer, and the author of the book *Sand Talk: How Indigenous Thinking Can Save the World*, a book that has clarified my thinking and been a huge influence on me. He is perhaps the most interesting philosopher I have ever talked to, but 'philosopher' feels like a very western word to put on him. He is a big thinker, a deep thinker and a thinker who genuinely is not bothered by what other people think of him.

I asked him what people are defined by and he connected it to a modern malaise before I had even mentioned unhappiness.

'Basically, you're an autonomous, fabulous individual. And your time is really important. And at the same time, it is severely checked into really balanced obligations, and relationships with your community, and to the place that you care for, to your relational tasks and obligations,' he says.

'So you have that dance, you're an autonomous individual, who is in a collective, which will be your family, and your family is an autonomous collective ... It's a tension and balance between your autonomy, your individual identity, and then your identity, it's almost impossible to separate from a collective identity. And we've always been this way, but that's not necessarily how people currently define themselves, that is completely different.

'People define themselves now by affiliations to different identity groups.'

He says what people are trying to define themselves by these days are their abstract identity categories – their gender, their sexuality, their ethnicity, their ability – but it's all wrong. Well, technically, they are right. Which is why people have to agree with them. He has to agree he is an Aboriginal man. I have to agree I am a straight woman. Because while these identity labels may be correct, they actually tell you nothing about ourselves. About what matters to us, who we love, what moves us, what makes us angry. The identity labels tell you nothing about who we are.

'You know, the Iceman up in the Alps, he didn't have a word for identity. A few thousand years ago, there *was* no word for identity, there wasn't a concept of identity, because identity was something that just was, you know. Part of the mess of identity now is because of abstraction. We try to divide these things into categories, and then think of ways to measure them,' he says.

'What your ideological brand is, that is what you're associating with your identity. So basically, we've had essentially consumer choices replace our actual identities. So all these little neoliberal subjects, each of us is a corporation unto ourselves. And our branding is key. Each of us has to make a lot of choices about pretty much every issue about, you know, how people can live, and what should be done. And every issue of group identities, all of your intersectionalities, all of your privileges and all of your under-privileges, everything. We make choices about them and there's like an algorithm, this aggregate of data points that make up your own little algorithm, which you get to curate in the world, and defend.

'And from that, you have a set of responses, and attack and defence points, that you need to police, and upgrade, and update rigorously and regularly. And you feel as though you have a voice, you feel as though you have some control in the world, as an agency within your environment, although you no longer live within an environment, you know, most of your environment is digital.'

What Tyson is talking about is people conflating who they are online with who they really are. That if some people feel they have the correct opinions and they post these opinions online, then they are a 'correct' person. But this idea that people have of themselves is an illusion. Even the idea that a lot of people have a voice now is an illusion. What really matters is our connection to our communities, our connections to the environment around us, to the land, and these connections are what a lot of people are being denied.

'Everybody has a voice, but nobody has an ear. So we're all screaming our identities into a void. Now we're basically building a patchwork quilt of an identity out of a series of abstracts that somebody else has made for us. Human identities are no longer grounded in place and relation, which is what we're supposed to be doing as a species as what we're patterned for, biologically and in every other way. So we're all experiencing quite intense genetic frustration signals about that at the moment, because, you know, we're missing our kin. All humans now are missing their kin,' he says.

'Without that kin, there is no identity. And if we were networked into that original, traditional, biological human identity, there would be no need for the abstract of abstracts, such as identity, anyway.'

Basically the recipe for misery is thinking too much about being a fabulous, autonomous individual and not enough about obligations to family, friends and community. The recipe for misery is not feeling connected to the place where we are living. Even thinking about what defines you, and therefore your identity, is not a very good means to an end, if the end is contentment.

'Why do we need to talk about our identity? Why do we need to think about it? It just is. It's about where you are and who you're in relation to, and what your roles and obligations are. How do you sit within the law of the land? How do you sit within the laws of obligation that you need to follow as a human being in order to even be a human?' Tyson says.

'What does it mean, if you do not even know that land or the law? And you're just drifting around? Not even an urban gecko. What does that mean for you, for your species? What does that mean for five, ten generations down the track? What are your descendants going to become? Because of your inability to relate? Because you are so fucking obsessed with your special identity? Either with mitigating its privileges, or temporarily cashing in on a moment where your intersectional under-privilege carries a small amount of social capital? A little bit of political cachet for the next five minutes. And believe me, that won't last.'

What will last is the stuff that matters in your life – your real life. The stuff in your life that matters is your connection to where you live, your community, your friends, your family. Not your job, your posts online or anything tied to status. If that is where you are looking for your identity, then you are going to feel very empty and wonder why. You are the people you love, your life is with your community.

**

Am I actually empathetic and a loose unit and responsible? I think I fool a lot of people into thinking I care more about these things than I actually do. I think when I am embarrassed by someone I love in public, I am actually embarrassed about what other people around us are thinking, while I myself truly don't give a shit that they've had two more glasses of wine than they should have. But who is telling the objective truth about me? Myself or someone who knows me?

It's meant to be a bit lame to admit you care so much about what other people think, but it turns out that is the lens pretty much everyone sees themselves through.

The stark truth is that all of these people reflecting yourself back to you, helping you define yourself – they are not actually spending that much time thinking about you. Whether you feel like you're achieving enough, or actually are achieving enough, or are a good person, or have decent motivations, this stuff really does not matter to many people.

The people who spend any real time thinking about you are yourself and probably your mum. Everyone else is busy with their own trivial stuff.

But if you want to be defined by something worthwhile, if it is important to you to at least be decent, then you have to do more than give a homeless woman with a broken leg $200. You have to keep trying to do the right thing. You don't get to be defined by one act; you don't get to be good because you did one good thing (remember, you could always have done more). You also have to do the good thing for the people you are closest to, not just strangers. You have to treat the people you love well, even when they are the most irritating people in the world.

But the good news is when you fuck it up, it doesn't make you a bad person either. You get to try again the next day. You get to keep trying to do the right and good thing the next day, and the day after that, and the day after that, and the month after that, and the year after that.

I thought my kid was dying and all I got was this lousy lust for life

When I was watching my son die, I did not behave in the way I had imagined I would in those grim games your mind sometimes forces you to play. Games such as, 'What would it be like if I was widowed?' 'What would it be like for my family if that bus hit me?' 'What would it be like if something terrible happened to my child?'

I actually only *thought* I was watching my son die, which is a big difference. My son is OK. But for that moment in time, there is no difference.

I cannot tell you the terror, you cannot imagine the terror, you don't know it unless you've felt it.

The other night, about half an hour after I got home, Hamish had a seizure. He is 16 months old and, from the day he was born (the day after his due date), he has been a robust little boy. There have not been many instances he has caused worry, aside from the usual constant low thrum of anxiety about SIDs/falling out of windows/anything at all happening to your beautiful little human.

My husband, Matt, and my brother, Séamus, were both home with me at the time, which was a stroke of fortune in the whole sorry saga. I am usually still at work at that time on a Tuesday, and my brother lives 25 minutes away but had stayed the day at our apartment in between night shifts at the local hospital. As I've mentioned, my brother is a nurse, more fortune.

Hamish was sitting in his highchair and I was half chatting to him while walking around, and Matt and Séamus were in the kitchen. Suddenly I saw Hamish's shoulder and head moving and knew something was so very wrong. I started screaming for Séamus, who rushed out of the kitchen with Matt. Séamus took one look at Hamish and yelled, 'Call an ambulance! CALL AN AMBULANCE!'

It had not occurred to me to call an ambulance. Previously I had thought I was the type to think to call an ambulance. It took all of my strength, effort and focus to dial 000 with my shaking hands and, as I stood crying on the balcony trying to say my address, I could see Matt and Séamus holding Hamish so he was draped forward over their arms and his airways were clear. They were both screaming his name while his eyes rolled back in his head and he continued jerking around.

I saw him turning blue.

'Ham! Ham! Stay with us! Ham!' There was something about how desperate my brother sounded as he yelled my son's name that made me think we were losing him.

As the 000 lady tried to give me instructions, I bent over, winded.

I thought we were watching him die.

I did not think much when I thought these were his last few moments with us. I probably just thought, 'This can't be real.'

In a way, it wasn't real. There was also the whispered begging deep inside me: 'Please, please. Take me instead. Take me.'

The woman on the phone snapped me out of it. 'You need to lie him down, are you listening to me? Can you hear me? You need to lie him down.'

I rushed over to the boys, all of my boys.

'Lie him down,' I managed to choke.

'I can feel his heart, I can feel his heart,' Matt was yelling.

Once we had laid him down, the seizure started to abate.

'Is he breathing? Ma'am, is he breathing? I need you tell me if he is breathing,' said the woman on the phone.

Again, it took everything in me to answer a question, to make an observation of something I had taken for granted every day. My kid breathing.

I could see his chest rising.

'Yes,' I retched. 'He's breathing.'

***

I had Hamish five months before I turned 30. It was a time in my life when everything was awesome. I'm not just saying how I felt about the time, it was an objective truth: my life was awesome. I had a book deal, I had my baby, I was in love, and I worked at the *Guardian*, all of which was beyond the wildest fancies 16-year-old me could have conjured for the future.

But over the next year, I found myself in and out of an ennui so clichéd it was embarrassing. I was looking around, thinking, 'I'm 30, this is a pretty good indicator of how my life is going to look. Is this the shape of my life?'

Is this it?

It may seem kind of stupid, but I had not considered that having a baby would close down some other options to me. That turning 30 would mean there were some things I was probably never going to do with my life. There were things I never wanted to do with my life that I didn't think about until I began to realise the doors were being closed, the windows becoming harder to reach.

I think every billionaire is a policy failure.

But suddenly I began to think, 'I'm probably never going to be mega-rich.' Billionaires live on a different planet to me. They don't go to the office every day. Weekends mean nothing to them. They don't have to save. They don't delay the grocery shop 48 hours for pay day. They don't have to do something as mundane as grocery shopping.

It took having a baby and turning 30 for me to properly realise it is unlikely I will ever be disgustingly rich. I'd never aspired to it, but there the fact is anyway: whether I had wanted it or not, I wasn't getting it.

I am from the 'Fuck the Queen and let the free birds fly' school, but probably nothing as exciting as what happened to Meghan Markle at age 35 is going to happen to me. Even if I do think Prince Harry is too stupid to marry, I have a kid now. I can't move to England with a kid.

***

A few days before Hamish had his seizure, terrorists bombed three churches and three luxury hotels in Sri Lanka on Easter Sunday. More than 250 people were killed. I had to force myself to read the news. All those parents not with their children as they died.

There's a line in a Kanye West track in which he talks about praying for Paris, as well as for the parents, in reference to the Paris terrorist attacks. I think he is talking about the parent of *every* victim, not just the little children. The parents of the teenagers, and the people in their 20s, and the people in their 50s. Pray for the parents getting those phone calls, getting those police visits to their doors.

There was a billionaire couple, Anders and Anne Holch Povlsen, who lost three of their four children in the bombings.

Three of their four children.

I read the accounts in a state of terror. How could they go on in the world? How little did it matter that they were billionaires? So little. It almost didn't matter at all now. A lot of what was most valuable to them did not exist in the world anymore.

I tried to imagine what it would be like to lose three of your children, to have one child left.

I have since learned that when you imagine what it is like to have what you love most in the world die in front of you, you are not really imagining what it is like. As a parent, you think you can maybe fathom what it is like to lose a child, but you cannot.

I do not subscribe to the parental philosophy that you don't know love until you have a child. There is a lot of bone-deep love in the world – for your mother, for your brother, for your wife, for your best friend of decades. There are other relationships, I'm sure, that are much more complex and devoted than the parent–child one.

But the love for your child is difficult to replicate. It is a love so big it can be suffocating. You witness something tiny and completely vulnerable come into the world, and become someone who can brush their teeth by themselves. That happens because you protected them and fed them and stayed up all night with them and watched them; and, on top of all that, they have your eyes.

It is a consuming, joyful, annoying type of love. It's a hard-work love and if something were to happen to them, it is not only an inconceivable hole in your life, but a lot of hard work gone.

I didn't think, 'That's a lot of hard work gone' when I thought my son was dying.

I'm sure the hard work would've crossed my mind later, though.

***

Hamish was exhausted for a few days after his seizure and then he recovered. He has never had a seizure since. In the days after, I could not leave him. I slept in the same room as him, I started crying when I was reading his books to him. I lost something fundamental to myself that day that I did not know was there. I used to be a cool and relaxed mum.

I realised I had had a secret but solid belief that my child could not die and now that is gone.

Matt, Séamus and I have never fully recovered. We now know what true terror feels like and we still shudder when we talk about that evening. It's so easy to take your child for granted, for the daily frustrations to build up, to view them as a nuisance. And then sometimes you are reminded of how big your love for them is, how fragile they are. I think it is so common for parents to be reminded of the preciousness of their children only when something bad happens, because you can't spend every day thinking about how humongous your love for them is. It's too big, it's too heavy and there are 1000 other things that need tending to rather than the thought of what your child means to you.

A hangover from the terror that I still suffer from is I see death everywhere. He could trip into the bucket of water in the garden and drown. A branch from that tree could suddenly break and fall on top of him. That car could mount the footpath. He could fall and crack his head open on those concrete steps at the beach. I could visualise his death every second day if I allowed myself.

I have to talk myself out of constant vigilance.

***

What happened to Hamish was a febrile convulsion. He had an ear infection that gave him a fever and the fever went up too quickly for his little body to handle, so he had a seizure. It is apparently common in children under five. The paramedic I rode in the ambulance with told me they have arrived at febrile convulsions and had to treat the parents before the child because of the state they are in. The paediatrician told me she hates watching children having seizures in a hospital setting, so she cannot think what it is like for parents at home with no knowledge of what it is.

***

I spent the weeks afterwards smelling Hamish's hair, appreciating his warm body, kissing him on the nose, lying in the bath with him, rejoicing in the way he pats his belly when I take his shirt off, doing the aforementioned random crying while reading him his boring books.

Is this it? I cannot believe I have a life so exquisite.

Séamus has since told me he didn't yell, 'Ham, stay with us', he yelled, 'Ham, I'm here, I'm here.'

Or at least he thinks he did.

We cannot remember.

How to like your life

There is so much to be unhappy about.

On a macro level: the ongoing global health pandemic, white supremacy, poverty, nepotism, the existence of billionaires, etc., etc.

On a micro level: personal disappointments, a boring job, no job, unhappy relationships, general uselessness, etc., etc.

A general malaise with life not working out the way you thought it would is another thing to add to the list of things you feel bad about, a trivial grievance. But this is your life. Constantly reminding yourself that there are starving children in Africa, that there are also people who have to suffer in ugly clothes in the world, is not the way to be happy. And your happiness is important.

When a friend of mine first read my writing on misery, he said to me, 'I don't see you in this, it doesn't feel honest.'

It was something that I had found troubling, because he was right.

I am happy.

I may have moments, or even months, of self-doubt and insecurity, but in my usual life I am happy. Very happy, even.

This is troubling because I feel it in direct opposition to my peers, as I gently judge them. It is time millennials were treated with a bit of rigour, but in all my interactions and spoken-out-loud thoughts I feel compelled to be kind (is that so bad really?), to say I understand, that it *does* suck, it is difficult, it is not fair. I feel a responsibility to so many of my peers who have failed to launch.

What is it about me that meant I have achieved the secure job, the loving relationship, the kids? I'm not extraordinarily intelligent (that is just a fact, no whiff of self-deprecation here, for once); I have the privilege of being white in Australia, but I come from an ordinary background; I did work hard, but I'm not convinced it was a huge amount harder than anybody else. I am doing better financially than my parents were at the same age, which is not the usual experience of millennials. The secret to that is to start from a low base and marry up.

I put a lot of it down to luck. It feels like luck because it doesn't feel earned. But what is luck but a gift, one you have to be open to accepting? Is there something in my temperament that makes it easier for me to take the good things that come my way? I do always have an expectation that things will work out. But I can't explain to people how to be happy like I am happy. Is my happiness to do with my expectations of the world? There are certainly things that have happened to me that have been awful, but I am not interested in excavating the worst parts of my life. I have expected it would work out and all that stuff has not ended up mattering much to me.

My happiness is to do with other people. The boundaries of my life are my relations with other people – my mum, my dad, my brother, my sisters, my husband, my sons, my best friends, my aunts, my uncles, my cousins, even my colleagues. It could be constricting, but it is hugely fulfilling, to have myself matter less, to have so much love.

I don't like when I am at the centre of anything, and I don't feel the need to be.

What my friend meant when he said I was dishonest was that I am a very content person. He was right that I am a content person, but my writing was not dishonest. Everyone has their dark nights of the soul; he was just getting a glimpse into mine. I cannot tell someone how to be happy like I am happy, but I can try to tell you some of the things I have learned.

I'm not going to pretend there are not neoliberal forces at play in your life that need overthrowing to create a better world and better lives for billions. But there are ways to feel better, things you can do in your day-to-day life that aren't overthrowing entrenched regimes. It's OK to want to feel happier.

At the beginning of the pandemic, I was so scared, terrified. I promised myself I would never take my puny life for granted again. Within a few months, I was complaining bitterly about a cool lipstick I had bought online taking six days to get delivered. To be fair, it was the perfect orangey red.

It is unrealistic to expect ourselves to walk around in a state of eternal gratitude. But it's important to be brought back to the vital stuff of life. The pandemic has at different times brought back the vital stuff of life to a lot of us, but the moment I thought my son was dying in front of me remains the most brutal way I have ever been brought back to it and is something I have never fully recovered from.

What is the vital stuff of life? A place to call home. The Cowboys winning against the Broncos. A big blue sky. A sunny Monday morning when you don't have to work. Fresh glasses of champagne with your best friends. The first spring swim in the ocean. The look on your dad's face when you pull into his driveway after months away. A perfectly cooked steak. Someone to hug. Milk chocolate. Good health.

If you look, there is a tiny joy every day of your life. There are also tiny irritations. You don't need to genuinely believe that your child is dying or that you might not see your sister for two years to see the tiny joys.

There is an exercise in stoicism: if you get tired of everything you possess, imagine you have lost all of these things. It is simple but effective. What would it be like if everything you had was gone? If you can think of this when deep in your misery, then it is a good way to be pulled out of it. What would it be like if the three people you love most in the world died? What would it be like if you had to leave your home? What would it be like if you were very ill? We can't always be looking to what we covet of other people's; we have to think what we have that others don't.

Better yet, try to stop thinking about yourself so much.

Having children is not obligatory for happiness, but one of the reasons it makes a lot of people happier, I think, is the relief of not thinking about yourself all the time. It's so good for you to put your desires second, and even third.

At least some of the time, we are all the main characters of our lives. It is more difficult than we readily admit to see other people as real. There are maybe just a handful of people in history who have been able to see other people as being as real as themselves. It's why so many books are written about parenting, about parents dying, about hedonistic 20s, about being 30, about the minutiae of life, as if it has happened for the first time. It's banal, domestic stuff until it actually happens to you and suddenly you realise how genuinely interesting it is. If you can devote some time and effort to other people, it is harder to be caught up in all the ways your life is going wrong, or how you think it is.

Thinking of other people, remembering the stoics, does not mean you should minimise your pain and suffering, however. Privilege, and the checking of it, is a popular pop culture concept at the moment. While it is good to recognise there is no such thing as a level playing field, that people born on third base should be reminded they didn't hit a home run, it shouldn't be used to lazily dismiss people. Pain is pain. Suffering is suffering. If you feel bad, then you feel bad. When someone else is having a hard time, it can be easy to check off their privileges, but the pain of other people is very real and it's important to see that. If you are going to accept your own pain, then you have to accept other people's too and try to sympathise.

When things are difficult, you can just acknowledge that life is going shit. But it will not be shit forever. Just as importantly, when things are going fantastic, remember, they will not be fantastic forever.

Just as Oliver Robinson told me, it would be very unnatural to be happy all of the time, throughout your one wild and precious life. If there is no misery, if you are not in a malaise, then why would you change anything? We need this miserable time.

We also don't need to be totally secure in our lives at all times, content in the knowledge we have made the best decision at every possible juncture. Maybe you *have* chosen the wrong apartment, the wrong partner, the wrong job or even ended up with the wrong kid. It's OK to wonder if you did, to try to change it, or, if you can't, to just make the best of it.

Defensiveness and insecurity creep into our discussions about the big life decisions, because we are expected to love all of our choices all the time. But sometimes the best choice for us, like whether to have children or not, does not feel good all of the time. It is freeing to accept your situation, accept you don't know if you made the wrong choice, accept you would like things to be different for the moment and then live with it.

You would probably not be happier if you had moved to a different city, if you had taken the higher-paying job, if your friends were slightly different. None of these things is what makes you happy, or what will pull you out of the 31-year-old malaise. It comes from accepting fewer options, that some things will not work out and others are going to blow up spectacularly. There will be grief, regrets, missed opportunities and you will say a lot of stupid things at nice parties. There are some things you can change about your life, but you also have to learn to accept that this is the way life is.

Or so I'm told anyway.

One of the biggest revelations for me out of the global health pandemic was how much was out of my control, and how much and how quickly life can change. (I was the first person to notice this, you see.) You can either develop an anxiety disorder with this knowledge or, after being paralysed by it, welcome it and try to live life a bit more deliberately.

The other revelation from the pandemic and being 31 was the usefulness of boredom. A diary that is suddenly bare, the days yawning out in front of you, a small child to entertain; it's all so overwhelming at the outset and then suddenly, two months in, comes the realisation: there are good bits. There are always good bits, but a particularly surprising one was the return of boredom. I had not been properly bored since I was a teenager growing up in the country in a house that was impossible to sneak out of.

In the boredom of the same house and the same yard, day after day in 2020, my mind wandered. I had imaginary arguments with people; I made up funny scenarios for my kid; I thought about what I would do in various elaborate tragedies; I made up jokes; I remembered things I hadn't thought about in years; I even talked a bit to my dead nana, my dead uncle and my dead aunt. My mind wandered and I found myself cultivating a rich inner life again, an internal world as vivid to me as the external one.

The benefits of boredom have long been espoused and many have raised concerns that our smartphones are killing boredom. I don't think it's the smartphones, however; it's pretty easy to get sick of them. It's the insane social diaries. The catch-up drinks, the playdates, the dinners, the barbecues, the constant activities. Our packed social calendars do more to push boredom to the edges than a device. A frenzied need to always be doing something, *anything*. Lockdown took all that away. A lot of us thought that after lockdown we would be back in the pubs hugging each other, but there was still a limited life to live. Pubs and restaurants did not open to full capacity, you couldn't stand up in them. There were limits on life for more than a year after the first lockdown. A limited life that felt much easier in some aspects (SOME).

When I used to take annual leave, my holiday would be booked for the first day of it and I would return two or three days before I was due back at work. When my husband was forced to take seven weeks of his long-service leave while in lockdown, we were both horrified. What would he do?

Pass the time in a pleasant way, it turns out. We just hung out. Even though I was working, our lives instantly became calmer. He cooked some elaborate meals and a lot of delicious basic meals, the groceries were always done, we watched movies, there was no mad rush for pick-up and drop-off, we went for evening walks, we had so many meandering conversations about nothing. There is so much to be said for just hanging out, sleeping, being a bit bored.

There is so much to be said for limiting your obligations to other people.

You can still help people and think of them, without being too obligated to them. Feel free to ignore them, even. If you are feeling overwhelmed by your phone, the emails, the group chats, the notifications in general, then feel free to just ... ignore them. You don't have to reply to someone just because they messaged you, and you certainly don't have to reply to them at the expense of your attention to the people you are with in real life.

This collective freak-out that hits at 31, it really can hit at any time. Where is my spouse? Where is my house? Where is my career? Where are my children? Is this life turning out the way I thought? It's caused by a myth about happiness: that it equals money, marriage, babies. It's one of the many tricks of capitalism for sure, but that doesn't mean it feels any less real. That we don't feel locked out or locked in. If you are unhappy in your life, a good question to ask yourself is, what would you do after you achieved the thing you are missing out on? Once you make enough money to live on – which is a vital factor, being able to live on how much you earn – how much more career success do you think you need before you would just stop? Or once you achieve your goal, do you have another goal in mind? Have you been tricked into striving?

One of my best and oldest friends, Rick, is also a writer. We met when I was 18 and he was 19, working as newspaper cadets on the Gold Coast. We were not very big on discussing dreams and ambitions; we were mostly too busy being shocked at our luck at landing jobs where we were paid to talk to people and write about it. But for both of us, a lifelong dream was to write a book, our deepest-held desire was to be an author.

Almost exactly 10 years after we met, we both got book deals within a few months of each other.

Out at dinner together, I asked him. 'Do you feel different?'

'No, not really,' he said straight away.

It is a question we kept asking each other over the months of book edits and publication.

'I thought this would feel different,' I said on the phone once. 'But I feel the same.'

'So do I,' Rick said. 'I thought it would be a bigger deal.'

We both agreed we were excited to have books coming out, but that was it. Some excitement, no revelatory and life-changing feelings otherwise.

We both loved our book launches – they were brilliant nights where we were surrounded by friends and family, basking in the attention and perceived success, getting drunk, signing so many copies of our real-life books that we wrote in real life. Rick's book went on to be a bestseller and was nominated for various awards. My book was a failure by those measures.

Our other friend got a book deal about a year after us, which also became a bestseller and then was optioned for a movie, with work starting on the script and an offer of production money from a particular company. He told us this in passing at a barbecue.

'Wow! That's incredible!' I said, slightly stunned. 'Are you thrilled?'

'Oh, well, yeah, I guess,' he said in a neutral tone. And I could tell he had been seduced by the same myth as Rick and I had. He had a bestselling book that could become a movie, and he was wondering why he wasn't happier.

At that point, I, with my failed novel, was the happiest in our little trio.

It turns out you can't just get a book deal and be happy. You can't just realise long-held career ambitions. You have to actually 'work' on 'yourself', not just external markers of success.

A list of times I felt happier than when I got my book deal:

- Chasing my son back to bed when he came out giggling at 10 pm saying he had been bitten by a crocodile
- Drinking my second glass of wine with my sisters, brother, mum and dad at Kirra Surf Club
- Waking up on a sunny Saturday morning in September without an alarm and hugging Matty
- When I stopped breastfeeding
- Sitting under a blue sky in a park with my best friend of more than two decades

- The beer at the end of the ten-kilometre Spit to Manly walk
- Watching *Happy Gilmore.*

One of the other myths of happiness, one of those completely made-up yardsticks to measure life by, is marriage. Or at least being in a relationship. Most people would assume that they would be happier if they were in a relationship; some people assume they would be happier if they were in a different relationship. While there are concrete adverse health effects of being too lonely, being single does not necessarily equate to loneliness.

In 2019, behavioural scientist Paul Dolan caused a minor scandal when he revealed at the Hay Festival that the happiest sub-group of people were single women without children. Men who were married were generally happier than single men, but straight married women with children were much more miserable.

'You see a single woman of 40, who has never had children – "Bless, that's a shame, isn't it? Maybe one day you'll meet the right guy and that'll change." No, maybe she'll meet the wrong guy and that'll change. Maybe she'll meet a guy who makes her less happy and healthy, and die sooner,' he said.

Dolan has the data to back it up and wrote about studies of misery and pleasure in his book *Happy Ever After: Escaping the myth of the perfect life.*

His comments went viral, with an outpouring of frustrated women thankful to have data for something they had long suspected, and of defensive straight men wondering what the agenda was.

It is not difficult for me to believe that married women with children are more miserable – if I had to do the majority of parenting, I would be miserable. I have a true co-parent, but I know I am the exception and not the norm. So if you want to be a straight woman happy in a marriage, maybe marry my husband specifically. Astonishing that it still needs to be spelled out: a fate worse than singledom is ending up tethered to the wrong person.

The right relationship could make you happier, but being single shouldn't be the source of your misery. What is scary about singledom for some people is it can feel like it is not chosen, whereas most married people, or people in long-term relationships, at some point chose to be with their significant other. (Whether it has worked out or evolved into a healthy relationship is another matter.) This doesn't quite bear out in the realities of being human – nobody chooses to be in an abusive relationship and people can end up feeling trapped by circumstances – but people often assume that singledom is more like bad luck than an active choice.

You can work to find a good partner, but you can't just choose to be in a great relationship – the variable of finding the right person is out of your control to some extent. Whereas, hypothetically, everyone could choose to be single.

The general malaise of the early 30s for so many seems to come down to not living up to myths perpetuated throughout our entire lives and increasingly precarious economic situations. We know money alone won't make you happy, but once you earn a liveable baseline, the happiness from it plateaus. This is such accepted wisdom it is basically a cliché. But I was still shocked to see it play out in my own life.

The financial year I turned 31, I earned $66,651. The following year, through a return to full-time work and money from various side projects, I came close to doubling that. I did not notice this until it was time to file my tax return. The doubling of my income in such a short amount of time seems like something that would have a big impact on my life, but not much in my life changed. My spending didn't change drastically, apart from the $900 a month on childcare fees. I ended up with the most money in my savings account that I've ever had in my life, and at tax time I realised I didn't know how much I was spending each month on Spotify and various news website subscriptions. That was the biggest change: I didn't have to watch my spending as closely, and if I wanted something I just got it. I bought more clothes than I usually would have and tried out some expensive moisturisers. But the way I felt? Well, that was pretty much the same. There was no change in my emotional equilibrium despite almost doubling my income.

Once we earn the baseline, it means we can relax; instead, we are being tricked into striving for the next tax bracket, working longer hours, thinking work can give our life meaning. Financial stability certainly plays a part in happiness, but a good career does not equal happiness. If you think that promotion is going to change your life, or having a different job with higher pay, or having a title you can brag about, then you are going to end up wondering why your interior life has not changed that much once you have achieved that goal. The most likely outcome is you will look to the next title, the next job, the next goal as the potential source of your happiness. It won't be there, either.

What you actually need is to be brought back to the vital stuff of life. A relationship? Maybe. Children? Perhaps. Friends? Almost certainly. Whether they are your chosen family or your actual family, having people who understand you, know you intimately, love you, is where you will find most of the pleasure in life.

One of the modern tricks in the myth of marriage is that it is the only place to find your shelter from the storm. Your husband or wife needs to be your closest friend, your only ally, the person you share all of your book and movie tastes with. This seeps into parenthood, specifically motherhood, too – once you have your children, they are then supposed to become the centre of your life; what was previously a hole inside you is now supposed to be filled with abundance. All the vital stuff of life cannot come from one person, however, whether you marry them, birth them, or are best friends with them.

There are various studies on the ideal number of friends. In my unscientific experience, I would put it anywhere between four and 24 friends. It varies all the time. You need friends who have known you a long time, friends who are in the same type of work as you, friends who read the same books as you and, most importantly, friends who you could tell anything to and won't judge you. These friends can also be your partner, your sisters, your cousins and your colleagues, but you need a few of them.

Talking to my friend about a possible move overseas to be with her partner, she wailed, 'I don't want him to be the only reason I move, his friends can't be my friends, I don't want to be unperceived!'

Most of what we all want out of our life is to be perceived. To feel known, and understood. To be treated as if we are a real person. To be unperceived is to have no real intimacy, to have people believe what we project into the world, instead of having people who can see right through us, know our context, are not afraid to pull us up.

One of the small things you can control in the world is how you see it. Is it something to be afraid of? Something to complain about? Somewhere where evil people lurk ready to do yourself and your family harm? Somewhere you continuously see people do dumb and annoying things, such as park their cars on footpaths and stand at the bottom of escalators blocking the way?

Or is the world something to be excited about? Somewhere you could be in love with, where people are mostly good and just trying to get through their day? Somewhere where there is something beautiful waiting on many corners if you just look? People are strange and fragile, try to take them as they are.

I know it is not as simple as that binary – like most people who have noticed oppression I have a white-hot rage deep inside me – but I do think it is useful to remember the world is not something to be in combat with. That there is joy.

If I contradict myself in these pages, it is because I contradict myself in my life. I change my mind all the time. I truly believe one thing as well as three other things that are in direct opposition to the original idea. In other words, I am just another normal person.

When I set out to write this book, it was on the assumption that today's 31-year-olds are the most miserable ever. But I was soon dispelled of that notion. I realised I was quite happy and also that I was not; I realised that I was caught between two impulses. But maybe the tension does not really need to be resolved.

It is authentic to feel dissatisfied and it is authentic to enjoy an ordinary life. There is not one unified authentic mood, so we need to give up looking for it. Instead, this book is about the tensions, the contradictions, the happy chaos many of us live in.

For millennials in particular, there has been a 'hard against it' narrative. Poor us. No houses, no long-term career, the world is burning. What we are up against in our 30s is tough. The rise (again) of fascism, a system rife with racism, COVID-19, class barriers, climate change, an increasingly unstable political climate in western countries, increasing inequality, ageing parents, frustrated personal ambitions, no milk in the morning for coffee.

But it is not the worst that anyone has ever faced; we are a lot more comfortable than the vast majority of people in human history. We don't have to be so passive. Life is not just a series of things that happen to you. Ultimately, you are the one who has to live your life, so what do *you* think about it?

We can't just be patted on the back and have our tears wiped away. There is some hard thinking to be done about the capitalist and environment-destroying systems we are complicit in, but also what we demand from the people around us. You can't just blame externalities; there is work that you have to be willing to do yourself, mostly *on* yourself. And the work is possible.

You can and should rage against the unfair systems at work in the way you live your life and try to make incremental changes. You can also derive pleasure from your existence, build meaningful relationships, try to value your time over more money, shower love on the people around you, spend your days noticing all the little things that make life extraordinary.

References

EPIGRAPH

Toni Morrison, 'The work you do, the person you are',
  New Yorker, 29 May 2017.

CHAPTER ONE

Stephanie Convery, 'I don't believe in astrology so why
  am I addicted to this horoscope app?', *Guardian
  Australia*, 30 May 2019.

Efrat Tseëlon, 'Introduction: A critique of the ethical
  fashion paradigm', *Critical Studies in Fashion &
  Beauty*, 2011, vol.2, no.1, pp.3–68.

Krithika Varagur, 'The skincare con', *The Outline*,
  30 January 2018.

**MARRIAGE IS AN EMPTY CONSTITUTION, AND
OTHER DUMB THINGS I'VE SAID**

Julia Baird, *Victoria, The Queen: An intimate biography
  of the woman who ruled an empire*, HarperCollins
  Publishers, Sydney, 2016.

Diane Singerman, 'The economic imperatives of marriage: Emerging practices and identities among youth in the Middle East', *SSRN Electronic Journal*, September 2007.

Cassie Werber, 'Being single in your 30s isn't bad luck, it's a global phenomenon', *Quartz*, 13 November 2018.

GRIEF AND MALAISE

David Marr, *My Country: Stories, essays & speeches*, Black Inc, Melbourne, 2018.

Martin Amis, *Experience: A memoir*, Random House, London, 2001.

Que Minh Luu, 'Joy will come again: Lessons from a life turned upside down', *Guardian Australia*, 18 April 2020.

I LIKE BEING ADDICTED TO MY PHONE

Jenny Odell, *How To Do Nothing: Resisting the Attention Economy*, Melville House, New York, 2019

Kevin Roose, 'Do not disturb: How I ditched my phone and unbroke my brain', *New York Times*, 23 February 2019

Tavi Gevinson, 'Who would I be without Instagram? An investigation', *The Cut*, 16 September 2019

José De-Sola Gutiérrez, 'Cell phone addiction: A review', *Frontiers in Psychiatry*, 2016, vol.7, no.175.

Nicola Davis, 'Study links high levels of screen time to slower child development', *Guardian*, 29 January 2019

Sheri Madigan, 'Association between screen time and children's performance on a developmental screening test', *JAMA Pediatrics*, 2019, vol.173, no.3, pp.244–250.

Rachel Becker, 'The problem with studies saying phones are bad for you', *The Verge*, 5 December 2018.

Lauren Oyler, 'Ha ha! Ha ha!', *The London Review of Books*, 2020, vol.42, no.23.

Andrew K. Przybylski, 'How much is too much? Examining the relationship between digital screen engagement and psychosocial functioning in a confirmatory cohort study', *Journal of the American Academy of Child & Adolescent Psychiatry*, 2020, vol.59, no.9, pp.1080–1088.

Jonno Revanche, 'Tumblr transformed me but now it's just another place for people protected from the mainstream', *Guardian Australia*, 2 May 2019.

Nyadol Nyuon, 'The real bullies who spread hatred and division aren't on Twitter – they're in plain sight', *Guardian Australia*, 27 February 2020.

The Australian Broadcasting Company Limited, *Year Book 1930*, 2nd edition, Commonwealth Publications Ltd, Sydney, 1931.

Chris Smyth, 'Doctors tell parents to cut children's screen time', *The Times*, 4 January 2019.

REASONS NOT TO HAVE CHILDREN

Rachel Cusk, *A Life's Work: On becoming a mother*,
    Fourth Estate, London, 2001.

REASONS TO HAVE CHILDREN

Heather Havrilesky, 'Should I have a baby?', *The Cut*,
    17 January 2018.

Taffy Brodesser-Akner, *Fleishman Is in Trouble*, Random
    House, New York, 2019.

MY MONEY AND MY ROUTINES

Marguerite Duras, *Practicalities*, Grove Press, New York,
    1992.

YOU DON'T HAVE TO ACHIEVE ANYTHING

Rebecca Solnit, 'The impossible has already happened:
    What coronavirus can teach us about hope',
    Guardian, 7 April 2020.

Taylor Lorenz, 'Stop trying to be productive', *New York
    Times*, 1 April 2020.

Charlotte Lieberman, 'Why you should stop being so hard
    on yourself', *New York Times*, 22 May 2018.

Drew Millard, 'There's no such thing as "productivity"
    during a pandemic', *The Outline*, 26 March 2020.

Olga Mecking, 'The case for doing nothing', *New York
    Times*, 29 April 2019.

Adam Grant, 'Productivity isn't about time management. It's about attention management', *New York Times*, 28 March 2019.

Jonathan Jones, 'Jim Carrey's art is yet more proof that Hollywood stars should avoid the canvas', *Guardian*, 10 August 2017.

Benjamin Kline Hunnicutt, 'Kellogg's six-hour day: A capitalist vision of liberation through managed work reduction', *Business History Review*, 1992, vol.66, no.3, pp.475–522.

TRAVEL DOES NOT MAKE YOU A BETTER PERSON
Ellen Whinnett, Stephen Drill, Andrew Koubaridis, Jane Hansen, Elise Williams, Rebecca DiGirolamo, Andrew Hough and AAP, 'Ruby Princess cruise ship nightmare: What went wrong and how it was doomed from the start', *Daily Telegraph*, 5 April 2020.

Muhammed Badamasi, 'Best practices can result in cultural cringe', YourCommonwealth, 27 March 2018.

Alison Carroll, '"Australia has no culture": Changing the mindset of the cringe', *The Conversation*, 8 November 2018.

Alana Schetzer, 'Australiana 2.0: How cultural cringe became cool', *Guardian Australia*, 2 June 2018.

A. A. Phillips, *On the Cultural Cringe*, Melbourne University Press, Melbourne, 2005.

Lorena Allam, '"Devastated" Indigenous owners say Rio Tinto misled them ahead of Juukan Gorge blast', *Guardian Australia*, 12 October 2020.

Jill Ker Conway, *The Road From Coorain*, Knopf Doubleday Publishing Group, New York, 1989.

DOES THE WAY YOU WERE PARENTED MATTER WHEN YOU HAVE SISTERS?

Samantha A. Sang, 'The effect of siblings on children's social skills and perspective taking', *Infant and Child Development*, 2017, vol.26, no.6.

Nina Howe and Holly Recchia, 'Sibling relations and their impact on children's development', *Encyclopedia on Early Childhood Development*, December 2017

W. Karmaus, 'Does the sibling effect have its origin in utero? Investigating birth order, cord blood immunoglobulin E concentration, and allergic sensitization at age 4 years', *American Journal of Epidemiology*, 2001, vol.154, no.10, pp. 909–915.

Judy Dunn, 'Sibling influences on childhood development', *Journal of Child Psychology and Psychiatry*, 1998, vol.29, no.2, pp.119–127.

Susan M. McHale, Kimberly A. Updegraff and Shawn D. Whiteman, 'Sibling relationships and influences in childhood and adolescence', *Journal of Marriage and Family*, 2012, vol.74, no.5, pp.913–930.

Robert Pomlin and Denise Daniels, 'Why are children in the same family are so different from one another?', *Behavioral and Brain Sciences*, 1991, vol.10, no.1, pp.336–338.

Amanda Hooton, 'How Sydney author Liane Moriarty sold six million books and inspired an HBO series', *Sydney Morning Herald*, 15 July 2016.

WHAT ARE YOU DEFINED BY?

Eleanor Gordon-Smith, *Stop Being Reasonable: How We Really Change Our Minds*, NewSouth Books, Sydney, 2019.

Tyson Yunkaporta, *Sand Talk: How Indigenous Thinking Can Save the World*, Text Publishing, Melbourne, 2019.

HOW TO LIKE YOUR LIFE

Sian Cain, 'Women are happier without children or a spouse, says happiness expert', *Guardian*, 25 May 2019.

Paul Dolan, 'The money, job, marriage myth: Are you happy yet?', *Guardian*, 6 January 2009.

Alison Arieff, 'Life is short. That's the point', *New York Times*, 18 August 2018.

Acknowledgments

Jeanne Ryckmans and Catherine Milne really saw what this book could be. It does not exist without either of you.

Thank you to Lara Wallace, a brilliant publicist, and Rachel Dennis, a brilliant editor. Andy Warren designed the cover and I am still delighted every time I see it.

Quite a few names have been changed in this book to protect privacy and other people's feelings. Thank you to everyone who gave me their time and thoughts.

Ricky Morton, Alyx Gorman and Elle Hunt let me pick their brains and gave me invaluable feedback on first drafts.

Adam Wesselinoff forced me to be a lot braver than I initially wanted to be.

Emily Lockwood and Pramita Karki gave me time to write by taking my kids.

Daisy Turnbull gave me a space to write.

Georgia Waters gave me a space to write and time to write and everything else. Especially everything else.

The people who were core to this project, probably without realising, just by being as smart as they are (that means I've taken something they've said and pretended I came up with it): Candice Gallimore, Emily Mulligan, SABINA HUSIC, Shannon Molloy, Tulsi Combe, Katherine Feeney, Tiger Webb, Eleanor Robertson, Ally Garrett and Jacqueline Maley.

My Guardian colleagues are a constant source of inspiration and support, and there are too many to name, so I will just thank everyone, but especially Svetlana Stankovic and Lenore Taylor.

I'd like to specifically not thank the following people who did nothing but try to distract me and lure me away from writing with better craic: Dan Nolan, Declan and Molly.

I'd also like to specifically not thank the great loves of my life, Hamish and Cormac, who only hindered me when it came to writing this book. My real life is with them.

I have so much gratitude for Mum thread and Australia's premier group chat.

I feel lucky every day to have my in-laws, Alan and Sharyn.

Dad and Mum – I can't believe it took me having children of my own to notice how extraordinary you both are! I can never thank you enough! Don't expect me to say it out loud very often though!

Thank you to the people who made me the person I am: Séamus, Anna and Alice Jabour.

And most of all, to Matty Q. You have made my world 14 times bigger and because of you I never have to solicit love in places I would never find it, like my work.